Revolution Song

Thomas Jefferson's
Legacy

Jim Strupp

Ashland Press
Summit, NJ

Pʊ

Revolution Song
Thomas Jefferson's Legacy
Copyright © 1992 Jim Strupp

Ashland Press
63 Ashland Road, Summit, New Jersey   07901

Library of Congress Catalog 92-096875
ISBN 0-9634710-0-7   93 - 106826

Printed by Practical Graphics, New York, New York
First Edition August 1992

14. 00 iii

For the Kids

"I have sworn upon the altar of God eternal hostility against every form of tyranny over the mind of man."

- Thos. Jefferson

Contents

Introduction

Thomas Jefferson, to many of our fellow citizens, is known hazily as one of our Founding Fathers, the author of the Declaration of Independence, and an early President of the United States. Most of our knowledge of him is derived from a history course taken long ago or an occasional reminder on the Fourth of July. Even his impressive memorial in Washington, D.C. seems to serve only as a reminder of a time long ago when speeches and writings of liberty were common and the giant, almost mythic figures that were our country's founders, strode upon the land.

But Jefferson was and is much more than the limited vision described above. He was America's true renaissance man. A passionate commitment to inquiry and the pursuit of knowledge marked his activities from early age. His accomplishments and contributions include the following:

- Eminent Attorney
- Member of the Virginia House of Burgesses
- Member of the Second Continental Congress
- Self-taught Architect
- Nationally respected Agriculturalist and Botanist
- Accomplished Violinist
- Conversant in five (5) languages
- Author of the American Declaration of Independence
- Governor of Virginia
- Minister to France
- Strong Philosophic architect of the French Revolution
- Secretary of State

- Author of the bill establishing religious freedom in Virginia
- Responsible for establishing the Nation's Capitol in Washington, D. C.
- Vice-President of the United States
- Author of the bill abolishing the importation of slaves into the United States
- Founder of the Democratic Party
- Consummated the Louisiana Purchase, doubling the size of our country
- Author of legislation providing for the access of free or cheap land for Americans
- Architect of plans for providing quality education for all American citizens.
- Strong instigator for the Bill of Rights in our Constitution
- President of the United States (Two Terms)
- Responsible for our decimal system of coinage and money
- Supporter and protector of Native Americans through realistic treaties which he always honored
- His personal library became the nucleus of our present Library of Congress
- With, his ex-law clerk James Monroe (fifth (5) President of the United States), helped author the Monroe Doctrine
- Founder of the University of Virginia

These accomplishments, awesome in their scope, would seem to guaranty his status as one of our most important historical figures.

Thomas Jefferson's real contribution, however, was that he was a renegade, a rebel, a revolutionary in the truest sense. His firm and unyielding belief that government and society should rest on the will of the individual and of the people, and his conviction that "life, liberty, and the pursuit of happiness" were natural rights guaranteed to all, regardless of their station in life, marked him in true contrast to most prevailing notions of the day.

Born with a slight lisp, he was not an effective speaker before large crowds. Yet, in his brilliant writings and within small groups, his strong, but well-mannered and well-constructed arguments usually carried the day. He was over 6'2" tall and towered over most of his contemporaries. Time and again he took on the monarchists, the monied interests, the state organized church, and the despots of his day to secure the fundamental rights of liberty and self-government for American citizens and their posterity. He rode his horse across the beautiful rolling lands of his beloved estate, Monticello, until the last year of his life. He died at age 83, on July 4th, 1826, fifty (50) years to the day of the signing of the Declaration of Independence. His co-libertarian, John Adams, died on the same day.

The small work that follows attempts to address, in Jefferson's own words, the enormous contribution he has made to us all. The notes of historical continuity that follow demonstrate how these revolutionary ideals have made their mark through succeeding generations.

His message of revolution for us today is clear and straightforward:

Protect your liberties and rights through personal involvement in the social and political process.

Question your leaders, representatives, the media and the press; don't take things for granted.

Respect the right of peoples in other countries to develop the principles of liberty and freedom in their own distinct way.

Fifty (50) percent voter turnout is an abomination and, if continued, will lead to loss of rights and representation.

Elect all representatives based on merit, not seniority.

True preservation and continued expansion of rights and liberties depends as much on introspection as external forces.

Trust in yourself, believe in your fellow man and extend to him the same love and liberties to which you aspire.

Jefferson was an eternal optimist. Though struggles, defeat and monumental battles marked most of his life, he believed in the future and the continuing perfectibility of the human spirit.

As he said many times, "everything will be alright."

Jim Strupp

August, 1990

Acknowledgments

Although the text of this little book reflects only the original writings of Thomas Jefferson, it is also the product of much help and cooperation.

First, thanks to my sister Kate Strupp Siegel for her support and encouragement. Another book will follow! Thanks to my wife Barbara for her patience in assisting me in editing.

Certain other works were immeasurably helpful for my thought process as well as providing quotations of Jefferson's work. They are: *The Home Book of American Quotations*, edited by Bruce Bohle, New York, Grammercy Publishing Co., 1986; *Rediscovering America's Values*, by Frances Moore Lappe, New York, Ballantine Books, 1989; *Documents of American History*, edited by Henry Steele Commager, New York, Appleton-Century-Crofts, Inc., 1958; *The Complete Jefferson*, assembled and arranged by Saul K. Padover, New York, Duell, Sloan & Pearce, Inc., 1943; *Thomas Jefferson: An Intimate History*, by Fawn M. Brodie, New York, W.W. Norton & Co., 1974; and finally special thanks to Richard K. Matthews whose excellent work, *The Radical Politics of Thomas Jefferson, A Revisionist View*, Kansas, University Press of Kansas, 1984, not only provided me with structure and ideas of content but clearly sets forth Thomas Jefferson as the revolutionary he truly was.

"... and the sign said the words
of the prophets are written on
the subway walls and tenement
halls ..."

Paul Simon, "Sounds of Silence"

◊

Declarations of Liberty

My God!, how little do my countrymen know what precious blessings they are in possession of, and which no other people on earth enjoy.

Equal and exact justice to all men ... freedom of religion, freedom of the press, freedom of person under the protection of the habeas corpus; and trial by juries impartially selected, — these principles form the bright constellation which has gone before us.

The cement of this Union is the heart blood of every American.

It is a comfort that the medal has two sides. There is much vice and misery in the world, I know; but more virtue and happiness, I believe.

Some men look at Constitutions with sanctimonious reverence, and deem them like the Ark of the Covenant, too sacred to be touched. They ascribe to the men of the preceding age a wisdom more than human, and suppose what they did to be beyond amendment ... Laws and institutions must go hand in hand with the progress of the human mind. ...We might as well require a man to wear the coat that fitted him as a boy, as civilized society to remain ever under the regime of their ancestors.

The republican is the only form of government which is not eternally at open or secret war with the rights of mankind.

I know no safe depository of the ultimate powers of society but the people themselves; and if we think them not enlightened enough to exercise their control with a wholesome discretion, the remedy is not to take it from them but to inform their discretion by education.

Governments are republican only in proportion as they embody the will of the people, and execute it.

No government can continue good but under the control of the people.

The qualifications of self-government in society are not innate. They are the result of habit and long training, and for these they will require time and probably much suffering.

Men, by their constitutions, are naturally divided into two parties: 1. Those who fear and distrust the people, and wish to draw all powers from them into the hands of the higher classe. 2. Those who identify themselves with the people, have confidence in them, cherish and consider them as the most honest and safe, although not the most wise, depository of the public interests. ... In every country these two parties exist ... The appellation of Aristocrats and Democrats is the true one, expressing the essence of all.

It is an axiom in my mind that our liberty can never be safe but in the hands of the people themselves.

We hold these truths to be self-evident, that all men are created equal.

Error of opinion may be tolerated where reason is left free to combat it.

It is error alone which needs support of government. Truth can stand by itself.

Were we directed from Washington when to sow and when to reap, we should soon want bread.

Were it made a question whether no law, as among the savage Americans, or too much law, as among the civilized Europeans, submits man to the greatest evil, one who has seen both conditions of existence would pronounce it to be the last; and that the sheep are happier of themselves, than under the care of wolves.

A strict observance of the written laws is doubtless one of the high virtues of a good citizen, but it is not the highest. The laws of necessity, of self-preservation, of saving our country when in danger, are of higher obligation.

That one hundred and fifty lawyers should do business together is not to be expected [as members of Congress].

The tree of liberty must be refreshed from time to time with the blood of patriots and tyrants. It is its natural manure.

The God who gave us life, gave us liberty at the same time.

The ground of liberty must be gained by inches.

We are not to expect to be translated from despotism to liberty in a feather bed.

No government ought to be without censors; and where the press is free none ever will.

Pride costs us more than hunger, thirst, and cold.

When we reflect how difficult it is to move or deflect the great machine of society, how impossible to advance the notions of a whole people suddenly to ideal right, we see the wisdom of Solon's remark that no more good must be attempted than the nation can bear.

Their seducers have wished war ... for the loves and fishes which arise out of war expenses.

Establish the eternal truth that acquiescence under insult is not the way to escape war.

We must meet our duty and convince the world that we are just friends and brave enemies.

You have not been mistaken in supposing my views and feelings to be in favor of the abolition of war ... I hope it is practicable, by improving the mind and morals of society to lessen the disposition to war; but of its abolition I despair.

There is ... an artificial aristocracy, founded on wealth and birth, without virtue or talents ... and provision should be made to prevent its ascendancy.

Inequality produc[es] so much misery to the bulk of mankind, legislators cannot invent too many devices for subdividing property ... .

... the dead have neither power nor rights over it [Property]. [Upon death] the portion occupied by an individual ceases to be his ... and reverts to the society ... [t]he child, the legatee or creditor takes it, not by any natural right, but by a law of the society ... Then no man can by natural right oblige the land he occupied ...

Wherein the will of everyone has a just influence ... the mass of mankind ... enjoys a precious degree of liberty and happiness.

Sometimes it is said that man cannot be trusted with the government of himself. Can he, then, be trusted with the government of others?

Some men are born without the organs of sight, or of hearing, or without hands. Yet it would be wrong to say that man is born without these faculties ... the want or imperfection of the moral sense in some men, like the want or imperfection of the senses of sight and hearing in others, is no proof that it is a general characteristic of the species.

... our attachment to no nation on earth should supplant our attachment to liberty.

We should be wanting to ourselves, we should be perfidious to posterity, we should be unworthy that free ancestry from which we derive our descent, should we submit with folded arms to military butchery and depredation, to gratify the lordly ambition, or sate the avarice of a British ministry.

[We shall continue] exerting to their utmost energies all those powers which our creator has given us, to preserve that liberty which he committed to us in sacred deposit and to protect from every hostile hand our lives and our properties.

Compare the numbers of wrongs committed with impunity by citizens among us with those committed by the sovereign in other countries, and the last will be found most numerous, most oppressive on the mind, and most degrading of the dignity of man.

Let me add, that a bill of rights is what the people are entitled to against every government on earth, general or particular; and what no just government should refuse, or rest on inference.

The tyranny of the legislatures is the most formidable dread at present, and will be for many years. That of the executive will come in turn; but it will be at a remote period.

If we cannot secure all our rights, let us secure what we can.

I think the best remedy is exactly that provided by all our constitutions, to leave to the citizens the free election ...

In Virginia ... at the first session of our legislature after the Declaration of Independence, we passed a law abolishing entails. And this was followed by one abolishing the privilege of primogenature, and dividing the lands of intestates equally among all their children, or other representatives. These laws, drawn by myself, laid the axe to the foot of pseudo-aristocracy. And had another which I prepared been adopted by the legislature, our work would have been complete. It was a bill for the more general diffusion of learning. This proposed to divide every county into wards of five or six miles square, like your townships; to establish in each ward a free school for reading, writing and common arithmetic; to provide for the annual selection of the best subjects from these schools, who might receive, at the public expense, a higher degree of education at a district school; and from these district schools to select a certain number of the most promising subjects, to be completed at an University, where all the useful sciences should be taught. Worth and genius would thus have been sought out from every condition of life, and completely prepared by education for defeating the competition of wealth and birth for public trusts.

We acted in perfect harmony through a long and perilous contest for our liberty and independence. A Constitution has been acquired, which, though neither of us thinks perfect, yet both consider as competent to render our fellow citizens the happiest and the securest on whom the sun has ever shone. If we do not think exactly alike as to its imperfections, it matters little to our country, which, after devoting to it long lives of disinterested labor, we have delivered over to our successors in life, who will be able to take care of it and of themselves.

◊

"In every child who is born, no
matter what circumstances and
of no matter what parents, the
potentiality of the human race is
born again and in him, too, once
more and of each of us, our
terrific responsibility toward
human life;   Toward the utmost
idea of goodness, of the horror of
terror, and of God."

James Agee,

"Let Us Now Praise Famous Men"

Education

Enlighten the people generally and Tyranny and oppressions of both mind and body will vanish like evil spirits at the dawn of day.

By far the most important bill in our whole code, is that for the diffusion of knowledge among the people. No other sure foundation can be devised for the preservation of freedom and happiness. If anybody thinks that kings, nobles, priests are good conservators of the public happiness, send him here [to Europe].

[Their European academies] commit their pupils to the theatre of the world, with just taste enough of learning to be alienated from industrious pursuits, and not enough to do service in the ranks of science.

If a nation expects to be ignorant and free, it expects what never was and never will be.

I have often thought that nothing would do more extensive good at small expense than the establishment of a small circulating library in every county, to consist of a few well-chosen books, to be lent to the people of the county, under such regulation as would secure their safe return in due time.

Man is an imitative animal. This quality is the germ of all education in him. From his cradle to his grave he is learning to do what he sees others do.

No nation is permitted to live in ignorance with impunity.

I very much suspect that if thinking men would have the courage to think for themselves, and to speak what they think, it would be found they do not differ in ... opinions as much as is supposed.

The good opinion of mankind, like the lever of Archimedes, with the given fulcrum, moves the world.

When the press is free and every man able entitled to read, all is safe.

... it is believed that the most effectual means of preventing this [tyranny] would be, to illuminate, as far as practicable, the minds of the people at large, and more especially to give them knowledge of those facts, which history exhibiteth, that, possessed thereby of the experience of other ages and countries, they may be enabled to know ambition under all its shapes, and prompt to exert their natural powers to defeat its purposes.

At every of those schools shall be taught reading, writing, and common arithmetick, and the books which shall be used therein for instructing the children to read shall be such as will at the same time make them acquainted with Graecian, Roman, English, and American History. At these schools all the free children, male and female, resident within the respective hundred, shall be intitled to receive tuition gratis, for the term of three years, and as much longer, at their private expense, as their parents, guardians, or friends shall think proper.

Be it enacted by the General Assembly, that on the first day of January, in every year, there shall be paid out of the treasury the sum of two thousand pounds, to be laid out in such books and maps as may be proper to be preserved in a public library, and in defraying the expenses necessary for the care and preservation thereof; ...

It appears to me, then, that an American, coming to Europe for education, loses in his knowledge, in his morals, in his health, in his habits, and in his happiness.

The natural course of the human mind is certainly from credulity to scepticism; ...

... much observation and reflection on these [educational] institutions have long convinced me that the large and crowded buildings in which youths are pent up, are equally unfriendly to health, to study, to manners, morals, and order.

I have long entertained the hope that this, our native State, would take up the subject of education, and make an establishment, either with or without incorporation into that of William and Mary, where every branch of science, deemed useful at this day, should be taught in its highest degree.

It is highly interesting to our country, and it is the duty of its functionaries, to provide that every citizen in it should receive an education proportioned to the conditions and pursuits of his life.

... the judge thereof shall appoint three discreet and well-informed persons, residents of the county, and not being ministers of the gospel of any denomination, to serve as visitors of the Elementary Schools in the said county; ... and shall proceed to divide their county into wards ... and ... shall propose to them ... — 1. the location of a school-house for the ward, and a dwelling-house for the teacher ... 2. the size and structure of the said houses ... At this school shall be received and instructed gratis, every infant of competent age who has not already had three years' schooling. And it is declared and enacted, that no person unborn or under the age of twelve years at the passing of this act ... shall, after the age of fifteen years, be a citizen of this commonwealth until he or she can read readily in some tongue, native or acquired.

And for the establishment of colleges whereat the youth of the Commonwealth may, within convenient distances from their homes, receive a higher grade of education.

A plan for female education has never been a subject of systematic contemplation with me. It has occupied my attention so far only as the education of my own daughters occasionally required. Considering that they would be placed in a country situation where little aid could be obtained from abroad, I thought it essential to give them a solid education, which might enable them, when become mothers, to educate their own daughters, and even to direct the course for sons, should their fathers be lost, or incapable, or inattentive.

The objects of ... primary education determine its character and limits. These objects would be.

> To give to every citizen the information he needs for the transaction of his own business;
>
> To enable him to calculate for himself, and to express and preserve his ideas, his contracts and accounts, in writing;
>
> To improve, by reading, his morals and faculties;
>
> To understand his duties to his neighbors and country, and to discharge with competence the functions confided to him by either;
>
> To know his rights; to exercise with order and justice those he retains; to choose with discretion the fiduciary of those he delegates; and to notice their conduct with diligence, with candor, and judgement;
>
> and, in general, to observe with intelligence and faithfulness all the social relations under which he shall be placed.
>
> ... And this brings us to the point at which are to commence the higher branches of education ... those, for example, which are,

To form the statesman, legislators, and judges, on whom public prosperity and individual happiness are so much to depend;

To expound the principles and structure of government, the laws which regulate the intercourse of nations, those formed municipally for our own government, and a sound spirit of legislation, which, banishing all arbitrary and unnecessary restraint on individual action, shall leave us free to do whatever does not violate the equal rights of another;

To harmonize and promote the interests of agriculture, manufacture, and commerce, and by well informed views of political economy to give a free scope to the public industry;

To develop the reasoning faculties of our youth, enlarge their minds, cultivate their morals, and instill into them the precepts of virtue and order;

To enlighten them with mathematical and physical sciences, which advance the arts, and administer to the health, the subsistence, and comforts of human life;

And, generally to form them to habits of reflection and correct action, rendering them examples of virtue to others, and of happiness within themselves.

Education generates habits of application, of order, and the love of virtue; and controls, by the force of habit, any innate obliquities in our moral organization. We should be far, too, from the discouraging persuasion that man is fixed, by the law of his nature, at a given point; that his improvement is a chimera, and the hope delusive of rendering ourselves wiser, happier or better than our forefathers were ... And it cannot be but that each generation succeeding to the knowledge acquired by all those who preceded it, adding to it their own acquisitions and discoveries, and handing the mass down for successive and constant accumulation, must advance the knowledge and well-being of mankind, not infinitely, as some have said, but indefinitely, and to a term which no one can fix or foresee.

What, but education, has advanced us beyond the condition of our indigenous neighbors? And what chains them to their present state of barbarism and wretchedness, but a bigoted veneration for the supposed superlative wisdom of their fathers, and the preposterous idea that they are to look backward for better things ... And how much more encouraging to the achievements of science and improvement is this, than the desponding view that the condition of man cannot be ameliorated, that what has been must ever be, and that to secure ourselves where we are, we must tread with awful reverence in the footsteps of our fathers ... nothing more than education advancing the prosperity, the power, and the happiness of a nation.

◊

"Come senators, congressmen
please heed the call

don't stand in the doorways,
don't block up the hall

... for the times they are a
changing."

Bob Dylan,

"The Times They Are A Changing"

Agriculture

Those who labor in the earth are the chosen people of God, if He ever had a chosen people, whose breasts He has made His peculiar deposit for substantial and genuine virtue.

Whenever there are in any country uncultivated lands and unemployed poor it is clear that the laws of property have been so far extended as to violate natural right. The earth is given as a common stock for men to labor and live on ... The small landowners are the most precious part of the State.

Agriculture, manufacture, commerce and navigation, the four pillars of our prosperity, are the most thriving when left most free to individual enterprise.

The wealth acquired by speculation and plunder is pugnacious in its nature and fills society with the spirit of gambling. The moderate and sure income of husbandry begets permanent improvement, quiet life, and orderly conduct.

The bank has just now notified it's proprietors that they may call for a dividend of 10. per cent on their capital for the last 6. months. This makes a profit of 26. percent per annum. Agriculture, commerce, & every thing useful must be neglected, when the useless employment of money is so much more lucrative.

To leave to others to bring what we shall want, and to carry what we can spare. This would make us invulnerable to Europe ... and would turn all our citizens to the cultivation of the earth; and, I repeat it again, cultivators of the earth are the most virtuous and independent citizens.

The cultivation of wheat is the reverse [not like tobacco] in every circumstance. Besides clothing the earth with herbage, and preserving its fertility, it feeds the labourers plentifully, requires from them only a moderate toil, ... and diffuses plenty and happiness among the whole.

[At Monticello] In the bosom of my family, and surrounded by my books, I enjoy a repose to which I have been long a stranger. My mornings are devoted to correspondence. From breakfast to dinner, I am in my shops, my garden, or on horseback among my farms; from dinner to dark, I give to society and recreation with my neighbors and friends.

My [Farming] rotation, ... is as follows:

1. Wheat, followed the same year by turnips, to be fed on by the sheep.

2. Corn and potatoes mixed, and in autumn the vetch to be used as fodder in the spring if wanted, or to be turned in as a dressing.

3. Peas or potatoes, or both according to the quality of the field.

4. Rye and clover sown on it in the spring. Wheat may be substituted here for rye, when it shall be found that the second, third, fifth, and sixth fields will subsist the farm.

5. Clover.

6. Clover, and in autumn turn it in and sow the vetch.

7. Turn in the vetch in the spring, then sow buckwheat and turn that in, having bundled off the poorest spots for cowpenning. In autumn sow wheat to begin the circle again.

I am throwing the whole force of my husbandry on the wheat-field because it is the only one which is to go to market to produce money ... the other fields are merely for the consumption of the farm.

We could, in the United States, make as great a variety of wines as are made in Europe, not exactly of the same kinds, but doubtless as good.

Several persons, farmers and planters of the county of Albemarle, having, during their visits and occasional meetings together, in conversations on the subjects of their agricultural pursuits, received considerable benefits from an inter-communication of their plans and processes in husbandry, they have imagined that these benefits might be usefully extended by enlarging the field of communication so as to embrace the whole dimensions of the State ... For these purposes we now constitute ourselves an agricultural society of the county of Albemarle ...

This, the natural progress and consequence of the art, has sometimes perhaps been retarded by accidental circumstances; but generally speaking, the proportion which the aggregate of the other classes of citizens bears in any state to that of its husbandmen, is the proportion of its unsound to its healthy parts, and is a good enough barometer whereby to measure its degree of corruption. While we have land to labor then, let us never wish to see our citizens occupied at a work-bench, or twirling a distaff. Carpenters, masons, smiths, are wanting in husbandry; but for the general operations of manufacture, let our workshops remain in Europe. ...The loss by the transportation of commodities across the Atlantic will be made up in happiness and permanence of government. ... It is the manners and spirit of a people which preserve a republic in vigor.

I have received, ... the medal of gold by which the society of agriculture at Paris have been pleased to mark their approbation of the form of a mould-board [A Plough] which I had proposed ... I receive with great thankfulness these testimonies of their favor, and should be happy to merit them by greater services. Attached to agriculture by inclination, as well as by a conviction that it is the most useful of the occupations of man, my course of life has not permitted me to add to its theories and lessons of practice.

I presume, like the rest of us in the country, you are in the habit of household manufacture, and that you will not, like too many, abandon it on the return of peace to enrich our late enemy, and to nourish foreign agents in our bosom, whose baneful influence and intrigue cost us so much embarrassment and dissension.

◊

"May God bless and keep you
always
May your wishes all come true
May you always do for others
and let others do for you
May you build a ladder to the
stars and climb on every rung
and may you stay forever young
May you grow up to be righteous
May you grow up to be true
May you always know the truth
and see the light surrounding
you
May you always be courageous,
stand upright and be strong
And may you stay forever young
May your hands always be busy
May your feet always be swift
May you have a strong
foundation when the wind of
changes shift
May your heart always be joyful
May your song always be sung
And may you stay forever
young."

                                   Bob Dylan,

                               "Forever Young"

Religion

Assuredly nobody will care for him who cares for nobody.

When angry, count ten before you speak; if very angry, an hundred.

Never suffer a thought to be harbored in your mind which you would not avow openly. When tempted to do anything in secret, ask yourself if you would do it in public. If you would not, be sure it is wrong.

I deem it the duty of every man to devote a certain portion of his income for charitable purposes; and that it is his further duty to see it so applied as to do the most good of which it is capable. This I believe to be best insured by keeping within the circle of his own inquiry and information the subjects of distress to whose relief his contribution should be applied.

Millions of innocent men, women and children, since the introduction of Christianity, have been burned, tortured, fined and imprisoned, yet we have not advanced one inch toward uniformity. What has been the effect of coercion? To make one-half of the world fools and the other half hypocrites.

To the corruptions of Christianity I am, indeed, opposed; but not to the genuine precepts of Jesus himself. I am a Christian in the only sense in which he wished any one to be, sincerely attached to his doctrines in preference to all others; ascribing to himself every human excellence, and believing he never claimed any other.

Of all the systems of morality, ancient or modern, which have come under my observation, none appear to me so pure as that of Jesus.

In extracting the pure principles which [Jesus]

taught, we should have to strip off the artificial vestments in which they have been muffled by priests, who have Travestied them into various forms, as instruments of riches and power to themselves ... there will be found remaining the most sublime and benevolant code of morals which has ever been offered to man.

The doctrines which flowed from the lips of Jesus himself are within the comprehension of a child; but hundreds of volumes have not yet explained the Platonisms engrafted on them.

Let us not be uneasy then about the different roads we may pursue, as believing them the shortest, to that our last abode, but following the guidance of a good conscience, let us be happy in the hope that by these different paths we shall all meet in the end.

Indeed, I tremble for my country when I reflect that God is just.

In every country and in every age, the priest has been hostile to liberty. He is always in alliance with the despot, abetting his abuses in return for protection to his own.

I never told my own religion, nor scrutinized that of another. I never attempted to make a convert, nor wished to change anothers creed. I have ever judged of others' religion by their lives ... for it is from our lives and not from our words, that our religion must be read.

[I am] a real Christian, that is to say, a disciple of the doctrine of Jesus, very different from the Platonists, who call me infidel and themselves Christian and preacher of the gospel, while they draw all their characteristic dogmas from what its author never said nor saw.

[I believe]

1. that there is one only God, and he all perfect

2. that there is a future state of rewards and punishments.

3. that to love God with all thy heart and thy neighbor as thyself, is the sum of religion

[We are all held together by] bonds of love, charity, peace, common wants and common aids.

... I say, for the human mind not to believe that there is, in all this, design, cause and effect, up to an ultimate cause, a fabricator of all things from matter and motion, their preserver and regulator while permitted to exist in their present forms, and their regenerator into new and other forms.

But it does me no injury for my neighbor to say there are twenty gods or no god. It neither picks my pocket nor breaks my leg.

If there be beyond the grave any concern for the things of this world, there is one angel who views their attentions with pleasure and wishes continuance of them while she must pity the miseries to which they confine me.

[Jesus'] parentage was obscure, his condition poor; his education null; his natural endowments great; his life correct and innocent; he was meek, benevolent, patient, firm, disinterested, and of sublime elequence ...[his doctrines] mutilated, misstated, disfigured by the corruptions of schismatizing followers ... frittered into subtleties and obscured with jargon [but Jesus' greatest contribution was that] He pushed his scrutinies into the heart of man; erected his tribunal in the region of his thoughts, and purified the waters at the fountain head.

[Clergyman have taken the true doctrines of Christ and] have compounded ... a system beyond the comprehension of man [To which Jesus] were he to return to earth, would not recognize one feature.

I am not afraid of the priests ... they have tried upon me all their various batteries, of pious whining, hypocritical canting, lying and slandering, without being able to give me one moment of pain.

When I was young I was fond of speculations which seemed to promise some insight into that hidden country [heaven] but ... I have for very many years ceased to read or to think concerning them, and have reposed my head on that pillow of ignorance which a benevolent Creator has made so soft for us ... I have thought it better, by nourishing good passions and controlling the bad, to merit an inheritance in a state of being of which I can know so little, and to trust for the future to Him who has been so good for the past.

Say nothing of my religion. It is known to my god and myself alone.

I am of a sect by myself.

In matters of religion, I have considered that its free exercise is placed by the constitution independent of the powers of the general government. I have therefore undertaken, on no occasion, to prescribe the religious exercises suited to it; but have left them, as the constitution found them, under the direction and discipline of state or church authorities acknowledged by the several religious societies.

Believing with you that religion is a matter which lies solely between man and his God, that he owes account to none other for his faith or his worship, that the legislative powers of government reach actions only, and not opinions, I contemplate with sovereign reverence that act of the whole American people which declared that their legislature should "make no law respecting an establishment of religion, or prohibiting the free exercise thereof", "thus building a wall of separation between church and state.

Difference of opinion is advantageous in religion.

They have made the happy discovery, that the way to silence religious disputes, is to take no notice of them.

The bishops were always mere tools of the crown.

God himself will not save men against their wills.

The life and essence of religion consists in the internal persuasion or belief of the mind. External forms of worship, when against our belief are hypocrisy ...

Truth will do well enough if left to shift for herself. She seldom has received much aid from the power of great men to whom she is rarely known and seldom welcome.

It is the refusing toleration to those of a different opinion which has produced all the ... wars on account of religion.

Difference of opinion leads to inquiry, and inquiry to truth ...

My opinion is that there would never have been an infidel, if there had never been a priest.

How much wiser are the Quakers, who, agreeing in the fundamental doctrines of the gospel ... and, keeping within the pale of common sense, suffer no speculative difference of opinion, any more than of feature, to impair the love of their breathern. Be this the wisdom of Unitarians, this the holy mantle which shall cover within its charitable circumference all who believe in one God, and who love their neighbor.

◊

"To my children

  ... Grow up as good
revolutionaries. Study hard so
that you can master technology,
which allows us to master
nature. Remember that the
revolution is what is important
... Above all, always be capable
of feeling deeply any injustice
committed against anyone,
anywhere in the world. This is
the most beautiful quality in a
revolutionary."

Che Guevara,

A Letter to His Children, 1965.

National Economy & Foreign Affairs

Peace and friendship with all mankind is our wisest policy and I wish we may be permitted to pursue it.

Peace, commerce and honest friendships with all nations, entangling alliances with none.

We owe gratitude to France, justice to England, good will to all, and subservience to none.

The less we have to do with the enmities of Europe the better. Not in our day, but at no distant one, we may shake a rod over the heads of all, which may make the stoutest tremble. But I hope our wisdom will grow with our power, and teach us that the less we use our power the greater it will be.

We must meet our duty and convince the world that we are just friends and brave enemies.

Our first and fundamental maxim should be never to entangle ourselves in the broils of Europe. Our second, never to suffer Europe to intermeddle with cis-Atlantic affairs.

At the time we were funding our national debt, we heard much about "a public debt being a public blessing"; that the stock representing it was a creation of active capital for the ailment of commerce, manufacture, and agriculture.

Never fear the want of business. A man who qualifies himself well for his calling, never fails of employment.

Our interest will be to throw open the doors of commerce, and to knock off all its shackles, giving perfect freedom to all persons for the vent of whatever they may choose to bring into our ports, and asking the same in theirs.

It accorded well with two favorite ideas of mine, of leaving commerce free, and never keeping an unnecessary soldier.

I have come to a resolution myself, as I hope every good citizen will, never again to purchase any article of foreign manufacture which can be had of American make, be the difference of price what it may.

Never spend your money before you have it.

I sincerely believe that banking establishments are more dangerous than standing armies, and that the principle of spending money to be paid by posterity, under the name of funding, is but swindling futurity on a large scale.

It is really more questionable than may at first be thought whether Bonaparte's dumb legislature, which said nothing and did much, may not be preferable to one which talks much and does nothing.

I hope we shall crush in its birth the aristocracy of our monied corporations which dare already to challenge our government to a trial of strength, and bid defiance to the laws of our country.

Every discouragement should be thrown in the way of men who undertake to trade without capital.

As it is impossible to prevent credit, the best way would be to cure its ill effects by giving an instantaneous recovery to the creditor. This would be reducing purchases on credit to purchases for ready money.

How happy a people we were during the War from single circumstance that we could not run in debt. This counteracted all the inconveniences we felt, as the present facility of ruining ourselves overweighs all the blessings of peace ... to secure all this he needs but one act of self denial, to put off buying anything till he has the money to pay for it.

New schemes are on foot for bringing more paper to market by encouraging great manufacturing companies to form, and their actions, or paper-shares, to be transferable as bank-stock. We are ruined, Sir, if we do not over rule the principles that "the more we owe, the more prosperous we shall be," "that a public debt furnishes the means of enterprise," "that if ours should be once paid off, we should incur another by any means however extravagant", etc.

The political economists of Europe have established it as a principle that every state should endeavour to manufacture for itself: and this principle, like many others, we transfer to America, without calculating the difference of circumstance which should often produce a difference of result.

In Europe the lands are either cultivated, or locked up against the cultivator. Manufacture must therefore be resorted to of necessity not of choice.

Shall we make our own comforts, or go without them, at the will of a foreign nation? He, therefore, who is now against manufacture, must be for reducing us either to dependence on that foreign nation, or to be clothed in skins, and to live like wild beasts in dens and caverns. I am not one of these; experience has taught me that manufactures are now as necessary to our independence as to our comfort.

[After the War of 1812] our enemy has indeed the consolation of Satan on removing our first parents from Paradise: from a peaceable and agricultural nation, he makes us a military and manufacturing one.

I trust the good sense of our country will see that its greatest prosperity depends on a due balance between agriculture, manufacture and commerce, and not in this protuberant navigation which has kept us in hot water from the commencement of our government.

War against Bedlam would be just as rational as against Europe, in its present condition of total demoralization. When peace becomes more losing than war, we may prefer the latter on principles of pecuniary calculation. But for us to attempt war, to reform all Europe, and bring them back to principles of morality, and a respect for the equal rights of nations, would show us to be only maniacs of another character. We should, indeed, have the merit of the good intentions as well as the folly of the hero of La Mancha.

[The] continuance of the Embargo for two months longer would have prevented our war [of 1812].

But if ever I was gratified with the possession of power, and of the confidence of those who had entrusted me with it, it was on that occasion when I was enabled to use both for the prevention of war, towards which the torrent of passion here was directed almost irresistibly, and when not another person in the United States, less supported by authority and favor, could have resisted it.

I hope we shall prove how much happier for man the Quaker policy is, and that the life of the feeder is better than that of the fighter.

Instead of embarrassing commerce under piles of regulating laws, duties, and prohibitions, could it be relieved from all its shackles in all parts of the world, could every country be employed in producing that which nature has best fitted it to produce, and each be free to exchange with others mutual surpluses for mutual wants, the greatest mass possible would then be produced of those things which contribute to human life and human happiness; the numbers of mankind would be increased, and their condition bettered.

It is not to the moderation and justice of others we are to trust for fair and equal access to market with our productions, or for our due share in the transportation of them; but to our own means of independence, and the firm will to use them.

For example, if the [tax] system be established on the basis of income, and his just proportion on that scale has been already drawn from everyone, to step into the field of consumption, and tax special articles in that, as broadcloth or homespun, wine or whiskey, a coach or a wagon, is doubly taxing the same article. For that portion of income with which these articles are purchased, having already paid its tax as income, to pay another tax on the thing it purchased, is paying twice for the same thing, it is an aggrievance on the citizens who use these articles in exoneration of those who do not, contrary to the most sacred of the duties of a government, to do equal and impartial justice to all its citizens. ... To take from one, because it is thought that his own industry and that of his fathers has acquired too much, in order to spare to others, who, or whose fathers have not exercised equal industry and skill, is to violate arbitrarily the first principle of association, "the guarantee to everyone of a free exercise of his industry, and the fruits acquired by it." If the overgrown wealth of an individual be deemed dangerous to the State, the best corrective is the law of equal inheritance to all in equal degree; and the better, as this enforces a law of nature, while extra-taxation violates it.

The introduction of very cheap wine ... would be a great gain to the treasury, and to the sobriety of our country.

Here are a set of people, for instance, who have bestowed on us the great blessing of running in our debt about two hundred millions of dollars, without knowing who they are, where they are, or what property they have to pay this debt when called on; nay, who have made us so sensible of the blessings of letting them run in our debt, that we have exempted them by law from the repayment of these debts beyond a given proportion (generally estimated at one-third). And to fill up the measure of blessing, instead of paying, they receive an interest on what they owe from those to whom they owe; ...

The overbearing clamor of merchants, speculators, and projectors, will drive us before them with our eyes open, until, ... our citizens will be overtaken by the crush of the baseless fabric [debt], without other satisfaction than that of execrations on the heads of those functionaries, who, from ignorance, pusillanimity or corruption, have betrayed the fruits of their industry into the hands of projectors and swindlers.

Coins [should be] arranged in decimal ration, they are within the calculation of everyone who possesses the first elements of arithmetic, and of easy comparison, both for foreigners and citizens, ...

... that when any person shall have invented any new and useful art, machine, or composition of matter or any new and useful improvement on any art, machine, or composition of matter, and shall desire to have an exclusive property in the same ... he shall be entitled to receive from the Secretary of State a certificate thereof ... to warn others against an interference therewith ...

Whatever Louisiana was, as retroceded by Spain to France, such exactly it is, as ceded by France to the U.S. by the treaty of Paris of April 30, 1803.

... I repeat it again, cultivators of the earth are the most virtuous and independent citizens.

[It is] "heresy against common sense and historical experience [that] a group of individuals, even the most intelligent and best-intentioned, would be capable of becoming the mind, the soul, the directing and unifying will of the revolutionary movement and the economic organization of the proletariat of all lands ... [the] learned minority [will create] a pseudo-representative government [which will] serve to conceal the domination of the masses by a handful of privileged elite"

"Michael Bakunin: Selected Writings",

Arthur Lehning, ed.

(London: Jonathan Cape, 1973)

Science

All eyes are opened or opening to the rights of man. The general spread of the light of science has already laid open to every view the palpable truth that the mass of mankind has not been born with saddles on their backs nor a few favored booted and spurred, ready to ride them legitimately, by the grace of god.

I believe we may safely affirm that the inexperienced and presumptuous bond of medical Tyros let loose upon the world destroys more of human life in one year than all the Robin Hoods, Cartouches, and MacHeaths do in a century.

The question before the human race is, whether the God of Nature shall govern the world by His own laws or whether priests and kings shall rule it by fictitious miracles.

As for France and England, with all their pre-eminence in science, the one is a den of robbers, and the other of pirates. And if science produces no better fruits than Tyranny, murder, rapine and destitution of nation morality, I would rather wish our country to be ignorant, honest and estimable as our neighboring savages are.

One of the questions you know on which our parties took different sides, was on the improvability of the human mind, in science, in ethics, in government, etc. Those who advocated reformation of institutions, pari passu, with the progress of science, maintain that no definite limits could be assigned to that progress. The enemies of reform, on the other hand, denied improvement, and advocated steady adherence to the principles, practices and institutions of our fathers, which they represented as the consummation of wisdom, and akme of excellence, beyond which the human mind could never advance.

This is not a world to live at random in as you do. To avoid these eternal distresses, to which you are for ever exposing us, you must learn to look forward before you take a step which may interest our peace. Everything in this world is a matter of calculation. Advance them with caution, the balance in your hand. ... Leave the bustle and tumult of society to those who have not talents to occupy themselves without them.

When nature assigned us the same habitation, she gave us over it a divided empire. To you [The Head] she alloted the field of science, to me [The Heart] that of morals. When the circle is to be squared, or the orbit of a comet to be traced; when the arch of greatest strength, or the solid of least resistance is to be investigated, take you the problem: it is yours: nature has given me no cognisance of it. In like manner in denying to you the feelings of sympathy, of benevolence, of gratitude, of justice, of love, of friendship she has excluded you from this controul. To these she has adopted the mechanism of the heart. Morals were too essential to the happiness of man to be risked on the incertain combinations of the head. She laid their foundation therefore in sentiment, not in science. That she gave to all, as necessary to all: this to a few only, as sufficing with a few.

I gather from his other works that he adopts the principle of Hobbes, that justice is founded in contrast solely, and does not result from the construction of man. I believe, on the contrary, that it is instinct, and innate, that the moral sense is as much a part of our constitution as that of feeling, seeing, or hearing; as a wise creator must have seen to be necessary in an animal destined to live in society.

On the contrary I hold (without appeal to revelation) that when we take a view of the Universe, in its parts general or particular, it is impossible for the human mind not to perceive and feel a conviction of design, consummate skill, and indefinite power in every atom of its composition the movements of the heavenly bodies, so exactly held in their course by the balance of centrifugal and centripetal forces, the structure of our earth itself, with it's distribution of land waters and atmosphere, animal and vegetable bodies, examined in all their minutest particles, insects mere atoms of life, yet as perfectly organised as man or mammoth, the mineral substances, their generation and uses, it is impossible, I say for the human mind not to believe that there is, in all this, design cause and effect, up to an ultimate cause, a fabricator of all things from matter and motion, their preserver and regulator while permitted to exist in their present forms, and the regenerator into new and other forms.

My proposition then, is, that our notation of money shall be decimal, ... that the Unit of this notation shall be a Dollar; that coins shall be accommodated to it from ten dollars to the hundreth of a dollar...

I learn with pleasure that the Philosophical Society has concluded to take in consideration the subject of a fixed standard of measures, weights ... and you ask for my ideas on it. ... The subject to be referred to as a standard, whether it be matter or motion, should be fixed by nature, invariable and accessible to all nations, independently of others, and with a convenience not disproportioned to its utility.

But in the subdivisons of general science, as has been observed in the particular one of natural history, it has been necessary to draw arbitrary lines in order to accomodate our limited views.

Disqualified by age and ill health from undertaking minute investigations, I find it will be easier for me to state to you my proposition of a lock-dock, for laying up vessels, high and dry, than to investigate yours ... I had a model of this lock-dock made and exhibited in the President's house, during the session of Congress at which it was proposed. But the advocates for a navy did not fancy it, and those opposed to the building of ships altogether were equally indisposed to provide protection for them ... Having no view in this proposition but to combine for the public a provision for defense, with economy in its preservation, I have thought no more of it since.

◊

"Thus American development has exhibited not merely advance along a single line, but a return to primitive conditions on a continually advancing frontier line, and a new development for that area. American social development has been continually beginning over again on the frontier. This perennial rebirth, this fluidity of American life, this expansion westward with its new opportunities, its continuous touch with the simplicity of primitive society, furnish the forces dominating American character."

Frederick Jackson Turner,

The Significance of the Frontier in American History

Native Americans

I am convinced that those societies (as Native Americans) which live without government enjoy in their general mass an infinitely greater degree of happiness than those who live under the European governments. Among the former, public opinion is in the place of law, and restrains morals as powerfully as laws ever did anywhere. Among the latter, under pretense of governing, they have divided their nations into two classes, wolves and sheep.

The principles of their [Native Americans] society forbidding all compulsion, they are to be led to duty and to enterprise by personal influence and persuasion ... the practical results from the circumstances of their having never submitted themselves to any laws, any coercive power, any shadow of government, their only controuls are their manners, and that moral sense of right and wrong, which like the sense of tasting and feeling, in every man makes a part of his nature.

He who made us would have been a pitiful bungler if he had made the rule of our moral conduct a matter of science. For one man of science, there are thousands who are not. What would have become of them? Man was destined for society. His morality therefore was to be formed to his object. He was endowed with a sense of right and wrong merely relative to this. This sense is as much a part of his nature as the sense of hearing, seeing, feeling. ... The moral sense, or conscience, is as much a part of man as his leg or arm.

Let a philosophic observer commence a journey from the savages of the Rocky Mountains, eastwardly towards our seacoast. These he would observe in the earliest stages of association living under no law but that of nature subsisting and covering themselves with the flesh and skins of wild beasts. He would next find those on our frontier in the pastoral state, raising domestic animals to supply the defects of hunting. Then succeed our own semi-barbarous citizens, the pioneers, in the advance of civilization, and so on in his progress he would meet the gradual shades of improving man until he would reach his, as yet most improved state in our seaport towns. This, in fact, is equivalent to a survey, in time, of the progress of man from the infancy of creation to the present day. I am eighty-one years of age, born where I now live, in the first range of mountains in the interior of our country. And I have observed this march of civilization advancing from the seacoast, passing over us like a cloud of light, increasing our knowledge and improving our condition, insomuch as that we are at this time more advanced in civilization here than the seaports were when I was a boy. And where this progress will stop no one can say. Barbarism has, in the meantime, been receding before the steady step of amelioration; and will in time, I trust, disappear from the earth.

I believe the Indian then to be in body and mind equal to the whiteman.

It will be said, that great societies cannot exist without government. The savages, therefore, break them into small ones.

It is to be lamented then, very much to be lamented, that we have suffered so many of the Indian tribes already to extinguish, without our having previously collected and deposited in the records of literature, the general rudiments at least of the languages they spoke.

The Indian of North America ... is brave, when an enterprise depends on bravery; education with him making the point of honor consist in the destruction of an enemy by stratagem, and in the preservation of his own person free from injury; or perhaps, this is nature, while it is education which teaches us to honor force more than finesse; that he will defend himself against a host of enemies, always choosing to be killed, rather than to surrender, ... also, he meets death with more deliberation, and endures Tortures with a firmness unknown almost to religious enthusiasm with us; that he is affectionate to his children, careful of them, and indulgent in the extreme; ... even the warriors weeping most bitterly on the loss of their children, though in general they endeavor to appear superior to human events; that his vivacity and activity of mind is equal to ours in the same situation, hence his eagerness for hunting and for games of chance.

Of their eminence in oratory we have fewer examples, because it is displayed chiefly in their own councils. Some, however, we have, of very superior lustre. I may challenge the whole orations of Demosthenes and Cicero, and of any more eminent orator, if Europe has furnished more eminent, to produce a single passage, superior to the speech of Logan, a Mingo chief, to Lord Dunmore, the governor of this State. And as a testimony of their talents in this line, I beg leave to introduce it, first stating the incidents necessary for understanding it. In the spring of the year 1774, a robbery was committed by some Indians on certain land-adventurers on the river Ohio. The whites in that quarter, according to their custom, undertook to punish this outrage in a summary way. Captain Michael Cresap, and a certain Daniel Greathouse, leading on these parties, surprised, at different times, travelling and hunting parties of the Indians, having their women and children with them, and murdered many. Among these were unfortunately the family of Logan, a chief celebrated in peace and war, and long distinguished as the friend of the whites. This unworthy return provoked his vengeance. He accordingly signolized himself in the War which ensued. In the autumn of the same year a decisive battle was fought at the mouth of the Great Kankaway, between the collected forces of the Shawanese, Mingoes and Delaware, and a detachment of the Virginia militia. The Indians were defeated and sued for peace. Logan, however, disdained to be seen among the suppliants. But lest the sincerity of a treaty should be disturbed, from which so distinguished a chief absented himself, he sent, by a messenger, the following speech, to be delivered to Lord Dunmore. 'I appeal to any white man to say, if ever he entered Logan's cabin hungry, and he gave him not meat; if ever he came cold and naked, and he clothed him not. During the course of the last long and bloody war Logan remained idle in his cabin, an advocate for peace. Such was my love for the whites, that my countryman pointed as they passed, and said, "Logan is the friend of white men." I had even thought to have lived with you, but for the injuries of one man, Colonel Cresap, the last spring, in cold blood, and unprovoked, murdered all the relations of Logan, not even sparing my women and children. There runs not a drop of my blood in the veins of any living creature. This called on me for revenge. I have sought it: I have killed many: I have fully glutted my vengeance: for my country I rejoice at the beams of peace. But do not harbor a thought that mine is the joy of fear. Logan never felt fear. He will not turn on his heel to save his life. Who is there to mourn for Logan? — Not one!

I have joined with you sincerely in smoking the pipe of peace; it is a good old custom handed down by your ancestors, and as such, I respect and join in it with reverance. I hope we shall long continue to smoke in friendship together ... Hold fast the chain of friendship which binds us together, keep it bright as the sun, and let them, you and us, live together in perpetual love.

Peace, brothers, is better than war ... On our part, we shall endeavor in all things to be just and generous towards you, and to aid you in meeting those difficulties which a change of circumstance is bringing on.

You remind me, brothers, of what I said to you, when you visited me the last winter, that the lands you then held would remain yours, and shall never go from you but when you should be disposed to sell. This I now repeat, and will ever abide by. ... In all your enterprises for the good of your people, you may count with confidence on the aid and protection of the United States, and on the sincerity and zeal with which I am myself animated in the furthering of this humane work. You are our brethren of the same land; we wish you prosperity as brethren should do. Farewell.

On the contrary, the lines established between us by mutual consent, shall be sacredly preserved, and will protect your lands from all encroachments by our own people or any others. We will give you a copy of the law, made by our great Council, for punishing our people, who may encroach on your lands, or injure you otherwise. Carry it with you to your homes, and preserve it, as the shield which we spread over you, to protect your land, your prosperity and persons.

I have long desired to see you. I have now opened my heart to you; let my words sink into your hearts and never be forgotten. If ever lying people or bad spirits should raise up clouds between us, call to mind what I have said and what you have seen yourselves. Be sure there are some lying spirits between us; let us come together as friends, and explain to each other what is misrepresented or misunderstood, the clouds will fly away like the morning Fog, and the Sun of friendship appear and shine forever bright and clear between us.

"How many years must some people exist before they're allowed to be free."

Bob Dylan,

"Blowin in the Wind"

Slavery

The whole commerce between master and slave is a perpetual exercise of the most boisterous passions, the most unremitting despotism on the one part, and degrading submissions on the other. Our children see this, and learn to imitate it; for man is an imitative animal ...

The parent storms, the child looks on, catches the lineaments of wrath, puts on the same airs in the circle of smaller slaves, gives loose to his worst of passions, and thus nursed, educated, and daily exercised in Tyranny, cannot but be stamped by it with odious peculiarities. The man must be a prodigy who can retain his manners and morals undepraved by such circumstances.

[Young slaves, once educated and freed] should be colonized to such place as the circumstance of the time should render most proper, sending them out with arms, implements of household and of handicraft arts, seeds; pairs of the useful domestic animals, etc., to declare them a free and independent people, and extend to them our allegiance and protection, till they shall have acquired strength.

In 1769, I became a member of the [Virginia] legislature by the choice of the county in which I live ... I made one effort in that body for the permission of the emancipation of slaves, which was rejected; and indeed, during the regal government, nothing liberal could expect success. Our minds were circumscribed within narrow limits, by an habitual belief that it was our duty to be subordinate to the mother country in all matters of government, to direct all our labors in subservience to her interests, and even to observe a bigoted intolerance for all religions but hers.

Under the law of nature, all men are born free, and
every one comes into the world with a right to his
own person, which includes the liberty of moving
and using it at his own will.

[George III] ... has waged cruel war against human
nature itself, violating its most sacred rights of life
and liberty in the persons of a distant people who
never offended him, captivating and carrying them
into slavery in another hemisphere, or to incur
miserable death in their transportation thither ...

I think a change already perceptible, since the origin
of the present revolution. The spirit of the master is
abating, that of the slave rising from the dust, his
condition mollifying, the way I hope preparing under
the auspices of heaven, for a total emancipation.

Deep rooted prejudice entertained by the Whites; ten
thousand recollections; by the blacks, of the injuries
they have sustained; new provocations; the real
distinction which nature has made; and many other
circumstances, will divide us into parties, and
produce convulsions which will probably never end
but in the extermination of the one or the other race.

And can the liberties of a nation be thought secure
when we have removed their only firm basis, a
conviction in the mind of the people that these
liberties are the gift of God? That they are not to be
violated but with his wrath? Indeed I tremble for my
country when I reflect that God is just: that his
justice cannot sleep for ever: that considering
numbers, nature and natural means only a
revolution of the wheel of fortune, an exchange of
situation, is among possible events: that it may
become probable by supernatural interference! The
Almighty has no attribute which can take sides with
us in such a contest.

The voice of a single individual ... would have
prevented this abominable crime [Slavery] from

spreading itself over the new country. Thus we see the fate of millions unborn hanging on the tongue of one man, and Heaven was silent in that awful moment.

What a stupendous, what an incomprehensible machine is man! Who can endure toil, famine, stripes, imprisonment or death itself in vindication of his own liberty, and the next moment be deaf to all those motives whose power supported him thro' his trial, and inflict on his fellow man a bondage, one hour of which is fraught with more misery than ages of that which he rose in rebellion to oppose. But we must await with patience the workings of an overruling providence, and hope that that is preparing the deliverance of these our suffering brethren. When the measure of their groans shall have involved heaven itself in darkness, doubtless a god of justice will awaken to their distress, and by diffusing light and liberality among their oppressors, or at length by his exterminating thunder, manifest his attention to the things of this world, and that they are not left to the guidance of a blind fatality.

This abomination [the slave Trade] must have an end, and there is a superior bench reserved in heaven for those who hasten it.

... I am also unwilling to sell negroes ... this unwillingness is for their sake, not my own; because my debts once cleared off, I shall try some plan of making their situation happier, determined to content myself with a small portion of their labour.

I find I am not fit to be a farmer with the kind of labor we have.

[Regarding freeing the Slaves] this enterprise is for the young ... It shall have all my prayers, & these are the only weapons of an old man.

Gradually, with due sacrifices a general emancipation and expatriation could be effected. But, as it is, we have the wolf by the ears, and we can neither hold him, nor safely let him go. Justice is on one scale, and self preservation the other.

the abolition of the evil [Slavery] is not impossible; it ought never therefore to be despaired of. Every Plan should be adopted, every experiment tried ... I leave its accomplishment as the work of another generation.

All eyes were opened, or opening to the rights of man ... that the mass of mankind has not been born with saddles on their backs, nor a favored few booted and spurred, ready to ride them legitimately, by the grace of God.

The abolition of domestic slavery is the great object of desire in those colonies, where it was, unhappily, introduced in their infant state. But previous to the enfranchisement of the slaves we have, it is necessary to exclude all further importation from Africa. Yet our repeated attempts to effect this, by prohibition, and by imposing duties which might amount to a prohibition, having been ... defeated by his Majesty's negative: thus preferring the immediate advantages of a few British corsairs, to the lasting interests of the American States, and to the rights of human nature, deeply wounded by this infamous practice.

No person hereafter coming into this country shall be held within the same in slavery under any pretext whatever.

Whatever may have been the circumstances which influenced our forefathers to permit the introduction of personal bondage into any part of these States, and to participate in the wrongs committed on an unoffending quarter of the globe, we may rejoice that such circumstances, and such a sense of them, exist no longer.

... In the very first session held under the republican government, the assembly passed a law for the perpetual prohibition of the importation of slaves. This will in some measure stop the increase of this great political and moral evil, while the mind of our citizens may be ripening for a complete emancipation of human nature.

I have been the instrument of doing the following things...the act prohibiting the importation of slaves.

The moment of doing it with success has not yet arrived, and ... an unsuccessful effort, as too often happens, would only rivet still closer the chains of bondage, and retard the moment of delivery to this oppressed description of men.

... we find among them [Blacks] numerous instances of the most rigid integrity and as many as among their better instructed masters, of benevolence, gratitude, and unshaken fidelity.

Whatever be their degree of talent it is no measure of their rights.

But I know also, that laws and institutions must go hand in hand with the progress of the human mind. As that becomes more developed, more enlightened, as new discoveries are made, new truths disclosed, and manners and opinions change with the change of circumstances, institutions must advance also, and keep pace with the times.

The Committee to whom was recommitted the report of a plan for the temporary government of the Western territory have agreed to the following resolutions .... that after the year 1800 of the Christian era, there shall be neither slavery nor involuntary servitude in any of the said states, ...

"tell the children the truth ...

we've been trodding on the winepress

much to long ..."

Bob Marley,

"Babylon System"

Sketches of Others

GEORGE WASHINGTON

I think I knew General Washington intimately and thoroughly; and were I called on to delineate his character, it should be in terms like these.

His mind was great and powerful, without being of the very first order; ... and as far as he saw, no judgement was ever sounder. It was slow in operation, being little aided by invention or imagination, but sure in conclusion. ... He was incapable of fear, meeting personal dangers with the calmest unconcern. Perhaps the strongest feature in his character was prudence, never acting until every circumstance, every consideration, was maturely weighed; ... His integrity was most pure, his justice the most inflexible I have ever known, no motives of interest or consanguinity, of friendship or hatred, being able to bias his decision. He was, indeed, in every sense of the words, a wise, a good, and a great man. ... His heart was not warm in its affections; but he exactly calculated every man's value, and gave him a solid esteem proportioned to it. His person, you know, was fine, his stature exactly what one would wish, his deportment easy, erect and noble; the best horseman of his age, and the most graceful figure that could be seen on horseback. ... In public, when called on for a sudden opinion, he was unready, short and embarrassed ... His time was employed in action chiefly, reading little, and that only in agriculture and English history .... For his was the singular destiny and merit, of leading the armies of his country successfully through an arduous war, for the establishment of its independence; of conducting its councils through the birth of a government, new in its forms and principles, until it had settled down into a quiet and orderly train; and of scrupulously obeying the laws through the whole of his career, civil and military, of which the history of the world furnishes no other example ... He has often declared to me that he considered our new constitution as an experiment on the practicability of republican government ... that he was determined the experiment should have a fair trial, and would lose the last drop of his blood in support of it. ... I do believe that General Washington had not a firm confidence in the durability of our government. He was naturally distrustful of men, and inclined to gloomy apprehensions; and I was ever persuaded that a belief that we must at length end in something like a British constitution, had some weight in his adoption of the ceremonies of levees, birth-days, pompous meetings with Congress, and other forms of the same character, calculated to prepare us gradually for a change which he believed possible, and to let it come on with as little shock as might be to the public mind ... I felt on his death, with my countrymen, that "verily a great man hath fallen this day in Israel."

NAPOLEON

The Attila of the age dethroned, the ruthless destroyer of ten millions of the human race, whose thirst for blood appeared unquenchable, the great oppressor of the rights and liberties of the world, shut up within the circle of a little island of the Mediterranean ... How miserably, how meanly, had he closed his inflated career! ... He should have perished on the swords of his enemies, under the walls of Paris.

But Bonaparte was a lion in the field only. In civil life, a cold-blood, calculating, unprincipled usurper, without a virtue; no statesman, knowing nothing of commerce, political economy, or civil government, and supplying ignorance by bold presumption. ... After destroying the liberties of his country, he has exhausted all its resources, physical and moral, to indulge his own maniac ambition, his own tyrannical and overbearing spirit. His sufferings cannot be too great.

ANDREW JACKSON

I feel much alarmed at the prospect of seeing General Jackson President. He is one of the most unfit men I know of for such a place. He has had very little respect for laws or constitutions, and is, in fact, an able military chief. His passions are terrible. When I was President of the Senate he was a Senator; and he could never speak on account of the rashness of his feelings. I have seen him attempt it repeatedly, and as often choke with rage. His passions are no doubt cooler now; he has been much tried since I knew him, but he is a dangerous man.

PATRICK HENRY

Patrick Henry was originally a barkeeper. He was married very young, and going into some business, on his accounts, was a bankrupt before the year was out... Henry appeared in Williamsburg, and applied for a license to practice law. There were four examiners [who] at once rejected his application [but] after much entreaty and many promises of future study, succeeded in obtaining his. He then turned out for a practicing lawyer. ... These and similar efforts soon obtained for him so much reputation that he was elected a member of the legislature. He was as well suited to the times as any man ever was, and it is not now easy to say what we should have done without Patrick Henry. He was far before all in maintaining the spirit of the Revolution. ... Although it was difficult when he had spoken to tell what he had said, yet, while he was speaking, it always seemed directly to the point. ...

He was a man of very little knowledge of any sort; he read nothing and had no books. ... He wrote almost nothing — he could not write ... he was a man of debate only. ... After all, it must be allowed that he was our leader in the measures of the Revolution, in Virginia. In that respect, more was due to him than any other person.

JOHN ADAMS

A seven months' intimacy with him here [in Paris], and as many weeks in London, have given me opportunities of studying him closely. He is vain, irritable, and a bad calculator of the force and probable effect of the motives which govern men. This is all the ill which can possibly be said of him. He is as disinterested as the being who made him: he is profound in his views; and accurate in his judgement, except where knowledge of the world is necessary to form a judgement. He is so amiable, that I pronounce you will love him, if ever you become acquainted with him. He would be, as he was, a great man in Congress.

BENJAMIN FRANKLIN

When the Declaration of Independence was under the consideration of Congress, there were ... expressions in it which gave offense to some members. ... I was sitting by Dr. Franklin, who perceived that I was not insensible to [their] mutilations. "I have made it a rule," said he, " whenever in my power, to avoid becoming the draughtsman of papers to be reviewed by a public body. I took my lesson from an incident which I will relate to you. When I was a journeyman printer, one of my companions, an apprentice hatter, having served out his time, was about to open shop for himself. His first concern was to have a handsome sign-board, with a proper inscription. He composed it in these words, 'John Thompson, Hatter, makes and sells hats for ready money,' with a figure of a hat subjoined; but he thought he would submit it to his friends for their amendments. The first he showed it to thought the word 'Hatter' tautologous, because followed by the words 'makes hats,' which show he was a hatter. It was struck out. The next observed that the word 'Makes' might as well be omitted, because his customers would not care who made the hats. If good and to their mind, they would buy, by whomsoever made. He struck it out. A third said he thought the words 'for ready money' were useless, as it was not the custom of the place to sell on credit. Everyone who purchased expected to pay. They were parted with, and the inscription now stood, 'John Thompson sells hats.' 'Sells hats' says his next friend! Why nobody will expect you to give them away, what then is the use of that word? It was stricken out, and 'hats' followed it, the rather as there was one painted on the board.

So the inscription was reduced ultimately to 'John Thompson' with a figure of a hat subjoined."

"If we want to spread the revolution of liberty round the world to complete and reconcile the other great revolutions of our day, we have to re-examine its moral content and ask ourselves whether we are not leaving liberty as a wasted talent and allowing other forces, not friendly to liberty, to monopolize the great vision of men working in brotherhood to create a world in which we can all live. But God is not mocked. We reap what we sow and if freedom for us is no more than the right to pursue our own self-interest — personal or national — then we can make no claim to the greatest vision of our society: 'the glorious liberty of the sons of God.' Without vision we, like other peoples, will perish. But if it is restored, it can be as it always has been the profoundest inspiration of our society, and can give our way of life its continuing strength."

Barbara Ward,

The Rich Nations and The Poor Nations

Politics, Philosophy and Revolution

When any one State in the American Union refuses obedience to the Confederation by which they have bound themselves, the rest have a natural right to compel obedience.

George Washington set the example of voluntary retirement after eight years. I shall follow it. And a few more precedents will oppose the obstacle of habit to any one who after a while shall endeavor to extend his Term.

Ignorance is preferable to error, and he is less remote from the truth who believes nothing, than he who believes what is wrong.

I find the pain of a little censure, even when it is unfounded, is more acute than the pleasure of much praise.

Take things always by their smooth handle.

This is the true character of the English Government, and it presents the singular phenomenon of a nation, the individuals of which are as faithful to their private engagements and duties, as honorable, as worthy as those of any Nation on earth, and yet whose government is the most unprincipled at this day known.

I have deemed it more honorable and more profitable, too, to set a good example than to follow a bad one.

A wise and frugal government, which shall restrain men from injuring one another, which shall leave them otherwise free to regulate their own pursuits of industry and improvement, and shall not take from the mouth of labor the bread it has earned — this is the sum of good government.

The whole of government consists in the art of being honest.

The only orthodox object of the institution of government is to secure the greatest degree of happiness possible to the general mass of those associated under it.

The care of human life and happiness and not their destruction, is the first and only legitimate object of good government.

History, by apprising [Men] of the past, will enable them to judge of the future.

History, in general, only informs us what bad government is.

Every honest man will suppose honest acts to flow from honest principles.

He who receives an idea from me, receives instruction himself without lessening mine; as he who lights his taper at mine receives light without darkening me.

I have the consolation to reflect that during the period of my administration not a drop of the blood of a single fellow citizen was shed by the sword of war or of the law.

There is not a single crowned head in Europe whose talents or merits would entitle him to be elected a vestryman by the people of any parish in America.

If any of our countrymen wish for a king, give them Aesop's fable of the frog who asked a King; if this does not cure them, send them to Europe. They will go back republicans.

The earth belongs to the living, not the dead.

Politics, like religion, hold up torches of martyrdom to the reformers of error.

In a government like ours, it is the duty of the Chief Magistrate. ... to endeavor, by all honorable means, to unite in himself the confidence of the whole people.

If a due participation of office is a matter of right, how are vacancies to be obtained? Those by death are few: by resignation none. Few die and none resign.

No duty the Executive has to perform is so trying as to put the right man in the right place.

I have never been able to conceive how any rational being could propose happiness to himself from the exercise of power over others.

The good sense of the people will always be found to be the best army.

To aim at such a navy as the greater European nations possess would be a foolish and wicked waste of the energies of our country-men. It would be to pull on our own heads that load of military expense which makes the European laborer go supperless to bed.

Every difference of opinion is not a difference of principle.

Your own reason is the only oracle given you by heaven, and you are answerable for, not the rightness, but the uprightness of the decision.

A little rebellion now and then is a good thing, and as necessary in the political world as storms in the physical.

A single zealot may become persecutor, and better men be his victims.

My principle is to do whatever is right and leave consequences to him who has the disposal of them.

That the persons of our citizens shall be safe in freely traversing the ocean, that the transportation of our own produce, in our own vessels, to the markets of our own choice, and the return to us of the articles we want for our own use, shall be unmolested, I hold to be fundamental, and the gauntlet that must be forever hurled at him who questions it.

Nothing gives one person so much advantage over another as to remain always cool and unruffled under all circumstances.

John Adams ... said ... Reason, Justice, and Equity never had weight enough on the face of the earth to govern the councils of men. It is interest alone which does it.

What is called style in writing or speaking is formed very early in life, while the imagination is warm and impressions are permanent.

The unsuccessful struggles against Tyranny have been the chief martyrs of Treason laws in all countries.

Resistance To Tyrants is obedience to God.

The time to guard against corruption and Tyranny is before they shall have gotten hold of us. It is better to keep the wolf out of the fold than to trust to drawing his teeth and claws after he shall have entered.

And if Wise be the happy man, as these sages say, he must be virtuous too; for without virtue happiness cannot be.

The wise know too well their weakness to assume infallibility, and he who knows most, knows best how little he knows.

Where every man is a sharer in the direction of his ward - republic, or of some of the higher ones, and feels that he is a participator in the government of affairs, not merely at an election one day in the year, but every day ... he will let the heart be torn out of his body sooner than his power be wrested from him by a Caesar or a Bonaparte.

Divide the counties into wards of such size as that every citizen can attend, when called on, and act in person ... and by making every citizen an acting member of the government, and in the offices nearest and most interesting to him, will attach him by his strongest feelings to the independence of his country, and its republican constitution ... These wards, called townships in New England, are the vital principle of their governments, and have proved themselves the wisest invention ever devised by the wit of man for the perfect exercise of self-government, and for its preservation.

The true foundation of republican government is the equal right of every citizen, in his person and property, and in their management ... Try by this, as a tally, every provision of our constitution, and see if it hangs directly on the will of the people. Reduce your legislature to a convenient number for full, but orderly discussion. Let every man who fights or pays, exercise his just and equal right in their election.

[No republic can maintain itself without] ... general education and the creation of wards .. little republics ...

The way to have a good and safe government is not

to trust it all to one, but to divide it among the many, distributing to everyone exactly the functions he is competent to ...

[The Ward-republic provides that] the whole is cemented by giving to every citizen, personally, a part in the administration of the public affairs.

No society can make a perpetual constitution or even a perpetual law. The earth always belongs to the living generation.

[Through ward-republics] the voice of the whole people would thus fairly, fully, and peaceably expressed, discussed, and decided by the common reason of the society.

... Unsuccessful rebellions indeed generally establish the encroachments on the rights of the people which have produced them. An observation of this truth should render honest republican governors so mild in their punishment of rebellions, as not to discourage them too much. It is a medicine necessary for the sound health of government.

And what country can preserve it's liberties if their rulers are not warned from time to time that their people preserve the spirit of resistance? Let them take arms. The remedy is to set them right as to facts, pardon and pacify them. What signify a few lives lost in a century or two? The tree of liberty must be refreshed from time to time with the blood of patriots and Tyrants.

The generation which commences a revolution can rarely compleat it.

Independence can be trusted nowhere but with the people in mass. They are inherently independent of all but moral law.

[In] the multitude ... vital elements of free

government, of trial by jury, habeas corpus, freedom of the press, freedom of opinion, and representative government [are almost] innate.

Every man, and every body of men on earth, possesses the right of self-government: they receive it with their being from the hand of nature.

Wherever the people are well informed they can be trusted with their own government; that whenever things get so far wrong as to attract their notice, they may be relied on to set them to rights.

Life, liberty and the pursuit of happiness ... a participator in public affairs.

If we are made in some degree for others, yet in a greater degree we are made for ourselves.

I like the dreams of the future better than the history of the past.

We both consider the people as our children, and love them with parental affection. But You love them as infants whom you are afraid to trust without nurses; and I as adults whom I freely leave to self-government.

The constitution and the laws of their predecessors extinguished them in their natural course with those who gave them being. This could preserve that being till it ceased to be itself, and no longer. Every constitution then, and every law, naturally expires at the end of 19 years. If it be enforced longer, it is an act of force, and not of right.

It is time therefore for us to lay this matter before his majesty, and to declare that he has no right to grant land of himself. From the nature and purpose of civil institutions, all the lands within the limits which any particular society has circumscribed around itself, are assumed by that society, and subject to their allotment only. This may be done by themselves assembled collectively, or by their legislature to whom they may have delegated sovereign authority: and, if they are allotted in neither of these ways, each individual of the society may appropriate to himself such lands as he finds vacant, and occupancy will give him title.

I am conscious that an equal division of property is impractable. But the consequences of this enormous inequality producing so much misery to the bulk of mankind, legislators cannot invent too many devices for subdividing property, only taking care to let their subdivisions go hand in hand with the natural affections of the human mind.

The earth is given as a common stock for man to labour and live on. If, for the encouragement of industry we allow it to be appropriated, we must take care that other employment be furnished to those excluded from the appropriation. If we do not, the fundamental right to labour the earth returns to the unemployed.

They will forget themselves, but in the sole faculty of making money, and will never think of uniting to effect a due respect for their rights.

We must make our election between economy and liberty, or profusion and servitude. If we run into such debts, as that we must be taxed in our meat and in our drink, in our necessaries and our comforts, in our labors and our amusements, for our callings and our creeds, as the people of England are, our people, like them, must come to labor sixteen hours in the twenty-Four, give the earnings of fifteen of these to the government for their debts and daily expenses; and the sixteenth being insufficient to afford us bread, we must live, as they now do, on oatmeal and potatoes; have no time to think, no means of calling the mismanagers to account; but be glad to obtain subsistence by hiring ourselves to rivet their chains on the necks of our fellow-sufferers.

I find the general fate of humanity here [in Europe] most deplorable. The truth of Voltaire's observation offers itself perpetually, that every man here must be either the hammer or the anvil.

And say, finally, whether peace is best preserved by giving energy to the government, or information to the people. This last is the most certain, and the most legitimate engine of government. ... After all, it is my principle that the will of the majority should prevail.

You will see that my objection to the Constitution was, that it wanted a bill of rights securing freedom of religion, freedom of the press, freedom from standing armies, trial by jury, and a constant habeas corpus act. Colonel Hamilton's was, that it wanted a king and a house of lords. The sense of America has approved my objection and added the bill of rights, not the King and lords ... no man is more ardently intent to see the public debt soon and sacredly paid off than I am. This exactly marks the difference between Colonel Hamilton's views and mine, that I would wish the debt paid tomorrow; he wishes it never to be paid.

Our Revolution commenced on ... favorable ground. It presented us an album on which we were free to write what we pleased. We had no occasion to search into musty records, to hunt up royal parchments, or to investigate the laws and institutions of a semi-barbarous ancestry. We appealed to those of nature, and found them engraved on our hearts. ... Nothing then is unchangeable but the inherent and unalienable rights of man.

To these effusions for the cradle and land of my birth, I add, for our nation at large, the aspirations of a heart warm with the love of country; whose invocations to heaven for its indissoluble union will be fervent and unremitting while the pulse of life continues to beat, and, when that ceases, it will expire in prayers for the eternal duration of its freedom and prosperity.

Notes of

Historical Continuity

The following pages provide a selected bibliography for those interested in becoming more familiar with the life and times of Thomas Jefferson and the interpretations of what he did, what he wrote, and what he means for us today. Students of his life and his contributions to our political philosophy should find these readings comprehensive and indicative of his original work as well as the wealth of research that has been completed on all aspects of his life.

Also we have included historical documents which illustrate the course of political thought and struggle from Jefferson's time to our own. Many are familiar in title but may be unread in their entirety by most. Professor Henry Steele Commager's fine work *Documents of American History* provides the source of many of those listed. However, several are relatively unknown, but are felt to be equally important in understanding the ongoing pursuit of liberty around the world. These documents were written by people of courage in times when courage was most required. They are, for the most part, about change. They deal with the struggle to make things better through change yet reflect a consistent reliance on those self-evident truths of mans equality and his inalienable right to life, liberty and the pursuit of happiness. Courage to change! As John F. Kennedy said in *Profiles in Courage*:

"In whatever arena of life one may meet the challenge of courage, whatever may be the sacrifices he faces if he follows his conscience - the loss of his friends, his fortune, his contentment, even the esteem of his fellow men - each man must decide for himself the course he will follow .... stories of past courage can define that ingredient - they can teach, can offer hope, they can provide inspiration. But they cannot supply courage itself. For this each man must look into his own soul."

Selected Bibliography

The Jefferson Bible: The Life and Morals of Jesus of Nazareth O.I.A. Roche, ed. New York, 1964.

Allison, John M. *Adams and Jefferson: The Story of a Friendship.* Norman, Okla., 1966.

Appleby, "What Is Still American in the Political Philosophy of Thomas Jefferson?" William and Mary Quarterly 39 (Apr. 1982): 287-309.

Arendt, Hannah. *On Revolution.* New York: Viking Press, 1963.

Beard, Charles A. *Economic Interpretation of the Constitution of the United States.* New York: Macmillan Co., 1913 and 1935.

Economic Origins of Jeffersonian Democracy, New York: Macmillan Co., 1915.

Beloff, Max. *Thomas Jefferson and American Democracy.* New York, 1949.

Bohle, Bruce. *The Home Book of American Quotations.* New York: Gramercy, 1986.

Brodie, Fawn M. *Thomas Jefferson, An Intimate History.* New York: W.W. Norton, 1974.

Commager, Henry Steele. *Documents of American History.* New York: Appleton-Century-Crofts, Inc., 1958.

Cooke, Jacob E. *Alexander Hamilton.* New York: Charles Scribner's Sons, 1982.

Cunningham, Noble E., Jr. *The Jefferson Republicans: The Formation of Party Organization, 1789-1801.* Chapel Hill, N.C., 1957.

Erikson, Erik. *Gandhi's Truth.* New York, 1969.

Fried, Albert, ed. *The Jeffersonian and Hamiltonian Traditions in American Politics.* New York, 1968.

Graham, Pearl N. "Thomas Jefferson and Sally Hemings," Journal of Negro History. XLIV (1961),

89-103.

Hamilton, Alexander; Jay, John; and Madison, James. *The Federalist.* Edited by Jacob E. Cooke. 1st paperback ed. Middletown, Conn.: Wesleyan University Press, 1982.

Heslep, Robert D. *Thomas Jefferson and Education.* New York, 1969.

Hofstadter, Richard. *American Political Tradition.* New York, 1948.

Honeywell, Roy J. *The Educational Work of Thomas Jefferson.* Cambridge, Mass., 1931.

(Jefferson), Isaac. "Memoirs of a Monticello Slave, as Dictated to Charles Campbell by Isaac," Rayford W. Logan, ed. Charlottesville, Va., 1951. Republished in Jefferson at Monticello, James A. Bear, Jr., ed. Charlottesville, Va., 1967.

Jefferson, Thomas. *The Life and Selected Writings of Thomas Jefferson* - Edited by Adrienne Koch and William Peden, New York, 1944.

Kennedy, John F., *Profiles in Courage.* New York, Harper & Row, 1956.

Koch, Adrienne. *The Philosophy of Thomas Jefferson.* Chicago; Quadrangle Books, 1964.

Lappe, Frances Moore. *Rediscovering Americas Values.* New York: Ballantine Books, 1989.

Lehman, Karl. *Thomas Jefferson: American Humanist.* Chicago, 1947.

Malone, Dumas. *Jefferson and the Ordeal of Liberty.* Boston, 1962.

Mathews, Richard K. *The Radical Politics of Thomas Jefferson, A Revisionist View.* Kansas, 1984.

Miller, John Chester. *The Wolf by the Ears: Thomas Jefferson and Slavery.* New York: Free Press, 1977.

Padover, Saul. *Jefferson.* New York, 1942.

Padover, Saul. *The Complete Jefferson.* New York: Duell, Sloan & Pearce, Inc. 1943.

Paine, Thomas. *Common Sense and the Crisis.* New York, 1960.

Peterson, Merrill D. *The Jefferson Image in the American Mind.* New York, 1960.

Prince, Carl E. "The Passing of the Aristocracy: Jefferson's Removal of the Federalists, 1801-1805," Journal of American History, LVII (1970), 563-76.

Randolph, Sarah N., comp. *The Domestic Life of Thomas Jefferson.* New York: Frederick Ungar Publishing Co., 1958.

Rossiter, Clinton. *Alexander Hamilton and the Constitution.* New York, 1964.

Sheehan, Bernard W. *Seeds of Extinction: Jeffersonian Philanthropy and the American Indian.* New York: Published for the Institute of Early American History and Culture at Williamsburg, Virginia, by W. W. Norton, 1973.

Smith, James Morton. *Freedom's Fetters: The Alien and Sedition Laws and American Civil Liberties.* 2 vols. Ithaca, N.Y., 1956.

Spurlin, Paul Merrill. *Rousseau in America: 1760-1809.* University: University of Alabama Press, 1969.

Tocqueville, Alexis de. *Democracy in America.* 2 vols. New York: Schocken Books, 1961.

Turner, Frederick Jackson. *The Significance of the Frontier in American History.* New York: H. Holt & Co., 1920.

Van Pelt, Charles E. "Thomas Jefferson and Maria Cosway," American Heritage, XXII (1971), 24-29, 102-3.

Ward, Barbara. *The Rich Nations and the Poor Nations.* New York: W.W. Norton & Co., 1962.

Williams, William A. *America Confronts a Revolutionary World 1776-1976.* New York, 1976.

Wills, Garry. *Inventing America; Jefferson's Declaration of Independence.* New York, Doubleday & Company, Inc., 1978.

Young, Alfred F., ed. *The American Revolution: Explorations in the History of American Radicalism.* Dekalb: Northern Illinois University Press, 1976.

Historical Documents

Declaration of American
Independence
July 4, 1776

Virginia Statute of Religious
Liberty
January 16, 1786

The Bill of Rights
November 3, 1791

Jefferson's First Inaugural
Address
March 4, 1801

The Gettysburg Address
November 19, 1863

The Nineteenth (19) Amendment
to the Constitution of the United
States
August 26, 1920

Declaration of Independence of
the
Democratic Republic of Viet Nam
September 2, 1945

Truman's Civil Rights Message

February 2, 1948

Universal Declaration of Human
Rights

December 10, 1948

Brown V. Board of Education of
Topeka

1954

Speech by Haile Selassie

February 28, 1968

A DECLARATION BY THE REPRESENTATIVES OF THE UNITED STATES OF AMERICA, IN GENERAL CONGRESS ASSEMBLED

JULY 4, 1776

When in the Course of human events, it becomes necessary for one people to dissolve the political bands which have connected them with another, and to assume among the Powers of the earth, the separate and equal station to which the Laws of Nature and of Nature's God entitle them, a decent respect to the opinions of mankind requires that they should declare the causes which impel them to the separation.

We hold these truths to be self-evident, that all men are created equal, that they are endowed by their Creator with certain unalienable Rights, that among these are Life, Liberty and the pursuit of Happiness.   That to secure these rights, Governments are instituted among Men, deriving their just powers from the consent of the governed, That whenever any Form of Government becomes destructive of these ends, it is the Right of the People to alter or to abolish it, and to institute new Government, laying its foundation on such principles and organizing it as most likely to effect their Safety and Happiness. Prudence, indeed, will dictate that Governments long established should not be changed for light and transient causes; and accordingly all experience hath shown, that mankind are more disposed to suffer, while evils are sufferable, than to right themselves by abolishing the forms to which they are accustomed. But when a long train of abuses and usurpations, pursuing invariably the same Object evinces a design to reduce them under absolute Despotism, it is their right, it is their duty, to throw off such Government, and to provide new Guards for their future security. —-Such has been the patient sufferance of these Colonies; and such is now the necessity which constrains them to alter their former Systems of Government. The history of the present King of Great Britain is a history of repeated injuries and usurpations, all having in direct object the establishment of an absolute Tyranny over these States. To prove this, let Facts be submitted to a candid world.

He has refused his Assent to Laws, the most wholesome and necessary for the public good.

He has forbidden his Governors to pass Laws of immediate and pressing importance, unless suspended in their operation till his Assent should be obtained; and when so suspended, he has utterly neglected to attend to them.

He has refused to pass other Laws for the accommodation of large districts of people, unless those people would relinquish the right of Representation in the Legislature, a right inestimable to them and formidable to tyrants only.

He has called together legislative bodies at places unusual, uncomfortable, and distant from the depository of their Public Records, for the sole purpose of fatiguing them into compliance with his measures.

He has dissolved Representative Houses repeatedly, for opposing with manly firmness his invasions on the rights of the people.

He has refused for a long time, after such dissolutions, to cause others to be elected; whereby the Legislative Powers, incapable of Annihilation, have returned to the People at large for their exercise; the State remaining in the mean time exposed to all the dangers of invasion from without, and convulsions within.

He has endeavoured to prevent the population of these States; for that purpose obstructing the Laws of Naturalization of Foreigners; refusing to pass others to encourage their migration hither, and raising the conditions of new Appropriations of

Lands.

He has obstructed the Administration of Justice, by refusing his Assent to Laws for establishing Judiciary Powers.

He has made Judges dependent on his Will alone, for the tenure of their offices, and the amount and payment of their salaries.

He has erected a multitude of New Offices, and sent hither swarms of Officers to harass our People, and eat out their substance.

He has kept among us, in times of Peace, Standing Armies without the Consent of our legislature.

He has affected to render the Military independent of and superior to the Civil Power.

He has combined with others to subject us to a jurisdiction foreign to our constitution, and unacknowledged by our laws; giving his Assent to their acts of pretended legislation:

For quartering large bodies of armed troops among us:

For protecting them, by a mock Trial, from Punishment for any Murders which they should commit on the Inhabitants of these States:

For cutting off our Trade with all parts of the world:

For imposing taxes on us without our Consent:

For depriving us in many cases, of the benefits of Trial by Jury:

For transporting us beyond Seas to be tried for pretended offence:

For abolishing the free System of English Laws in a neighbouring Province, establishing therein an Arbitrary government, and enlarging its Boundaries so as to render it at once an example and fit instrument for introducing the same absolute rule into these Colonies:

For taking away our Charters, abolishing our most valuable Laws, and altering fundamentally the Forms of our Governments:

For suspending our own Legislature, and declaring themselves invested with Power to legislate for us in all cases whatsoever.

He has abdicated Government here, by declaring us out of his Protection and waging War against us.

He has plundered our seas, ravaged our Coasts, burnt our towns, and destroyed the lives of our people.

He is at this time transporting large armies of foreign mercenaries to compleat the works of death, desolation and tyranny, already begun with circumstances of Cruelty & perfidy scarcely paralleled in the most barbarous ages, and totally unworthy the Head of a civilized nation.

He has constrained our fellow Citizens taken Captive on the high Seas to bear Arms against their Country, to become the executioners of their friends and Brethren, or to fall themselves by their Hands.

He has excited domestic insurrections amongst us, and has endeavoured to bring on the inhabitants of our frontier, the merciless Indian Savages, whose known rule of warfare, is an undistinguished destruction of all ages, sexes and conditions.

In every stage of these Oppressions We have Petioned for Redress in the most humble terms: Our repeated Petitions have been answered only by repeated injury. A Prince, whose character is thus marked by every act which may define a Tyrant, is unfit to be the ruler of a free People.

Nor have We been wanting in attention to our British brethren. We have warned them from time to time of attempts by their legislature to extend an unwarrantable jurisdiction over us. We have reminded them of the circumstances of our emigration and settlement here. We have appealed to their native justice and magnanimity, and we have conjured them by the ties of our common kindred to disavow these usurpations, which, would inevitably interrupt our connections and correspondence. They too have been deaf to the voice of justice and of consanguinity. We must, therefore, acquiesce in the necessity, which denounces our Separation, and hold them, as we hold the rest of mankind, Enemies in War, in Peace Friends.

We, therefore, the Representatives of the united States of America, in General Congress, Assembled, appealing to the Supreme Judge of the world for the rectitude of our intentions, do, in the Name, and by Authority of the good People of these Colonies, solemnly publish and declare, That these United Colonies are, and of Right ought to be Free and Independent States; that they are Absolved from all Allegiance to the British Crown, and that all political connection between them and the State of Great Britain, is and ought to be totally dissolved; and that as Free and Independent States, they have full Power to levy War, conclude Peace, contract Alliances, establish Commerce, and to do all other Acts and Things which Independent States may of right do. And for the support of this Declaration, with a firm reliance on the Protection of Divine Providence, we mutually pledge to each other our Lives, our Fortunes and our sacred Honor.

JOHN HANCOCK.

New Hampshire

Josiah Barlett,

Wm. Whipple,

Matthew Thornton.

New York

Wm. Floyd,

Phil. Livingston,

Frans. Lewis,

Lewis Morris.

Massachusetts-Bay
Saml. Adams,
John Adams,
Robt. Treat Paine,
Elbridge Gerry.

Rhode Island
Step. Hopkins,
William Ellery.

Connecticut
Roger Sherman,
Sam'el Huntington,
Wm. Williams
Oliver Wolcott.

Georgia
Button Gwinnett,
Lyman Hall,
Geo. Walton.

Maryland
Samuel Chase,
Wm. Paca,

Thos. Stone,

Charles Carroll of Carrollton.

Pennsylvania
Robt. Morris,
Benjamin Rush,
Benja. Franklin,
John Morton,
Geo. Clymer,
Jas. Smith,
Geo. Taylor,
James Wilson,
Geo. Ross.

Delaware
Ceasar Rodney,
Geo. Read,
Tho. M'Kean.

North Carolina
Wm. Hooper,
Joseph Hewes,
John Penn.

South Carolina
Edward Rutledge,
Thos. Heyward, Junr.,
Thomas Lynch, Junr.,
Arthur Middleton.

Virginia

George Wythe,

Th. Jefferson,

Benja. Harrison

Ths. Nelson, Jr.,

Francis Lightfoot Lee,

Carter Braxton.

New Jersey

Richd. Stockton,

Jno.Witherspoon,

Fras. Hopkinson,

John Hart,

Abra. Clark.

VIRGINIA STATUTE OF RELIGIOUS LIBERTY
January 16, 1786

An Act for establishing Religious Freedom.

I. WHEREAS Almighty God hath created the mind free; that all attempts to influence it by temporal punishments or burdens, or by civil incapacitation, tend only to beget habits of hypocrisy and meanness, and are a departure from the plan of the Holy author of our religion, who being Lord both of body and mind, yet chose not to propagate it by coercions on either, as was in his Almighty power to do; that the impious presumption of legislators and rulers, civil as well as ecclesiastical, who being themselves but fallible and uninspired men, have assumed dominion over the faith of others, setting up their own opinions and modes of thinking as the only true and infallible, and as such endeavouring to impose them on others, hath established and maintained false religions over the greatest part of the world, and through all time; that to compel a man to furnish contributions of money for the propagation of opinions which he disbelieves, is sinful and tyrannical; that even the forcing him to support this or that teacher of his own religious persuasion, is depriving him of the comfortable liberty of giving his contributions to the particular pastor whose morals he would make his pattern, and whose powers he feels most persuasive to righteousness, and is withdrawing form the ministry those temporary rewards, which proceeding from an approbation of their personal conduct, are an additional incitement to earnest and unremitting labours for the instruction of mankind; that our civil rights have no dependence on our religious opinions, any more than our opinions in physics or geometry; that therefore the proscribing any citizen as unworthy the public confidence by laying upon him an incapacity of being called to offices of trust and emolument, unless he profess or renounce this or that religious opinion, is depriving him injuriously of those privileges and advantages to which in common with his fellow citizens he has a natural right, that it tends only to corrupt the principles of that religion it is meant to encourage, by bribing with a monopoly of worldly honours and emoluments, those who will externally profess and conform to it; that though indeed these are criminal who do not withstand such temptation, yet neither are those innocent who lay the bait in their way; that to suffer the civil magistrate to intrude his powers into the field of opinion, and to restrain the profession of propagation of principles on supposition of their ill tendency, is a dangerous fallacy, which at once destroys all religious liberty, because he being of course judge of that tendency will make his opinions the rule of judgment, and approve or condemn the sentiments of others only as they shall square with or differ from his own; that it is time enough for the rightful purposes of civil government, for its officers to interfere when principles break out into overt acts against peace and good order; and finally that truth is great and will prevail if left to herself, that she is the proper and sufficient antagonist to error, and has nothing to fear from the conflict, unless by human interposition disarmed of her natural weapons, free argument and debate, errors ceasing to be dangerous when it is permitted freely to contradict them.

II. Be it enacted by the General Assembly, that no man shall be compelled to frequent or support any religious worship, place or ministry whatsoever, nor shall be enforced, restrained, molested, or burdened in his body or goods, nor shall otherwise suffer on account of his religious opinions of belief; but that all men shall be free to profess, and by argument to maintain, their opinion in matters of religion, and that the same shall in no wise diminish, enlarge or effect their civil capacities.

III. And though we well know that this assembly, elected by the people for the ordinary purposes of legislation only, have no power to restrain the acts of succeeding assemblies, constituted with powers equal to our own, and that therefore to declare this act to be irrevocable would be of no effect in law; yet as we are free to declare, and do declare, that the rights hereby asserted that if any act shall hereafter be passed to repeal the present, or to narrow its operation, such act will be an infringement of natural right.

The Bill of Rights
(The First Ten Amendments to the Constitution of the United States Effective November 3, 1791)

Art. I

Congress shall make no law respecting an establishment of religion, or prohibiting the free exercise thereof; or abridging the freedom of speech, or of the press; or the right of the people peaceably to assemble, and to petition the government for a redress of grievances.

Art. II

A well regulated Militia, being necessary to the security of a free State, the right of the people to keep and bear Arms, shall not be infringed.

Art. III

No soldier shall, in time of peace be quartered in any house, without the consent of the Owner, nor in time of war, but in a manner to be prescribed by law.

Art. IV

The right of the people to be secure in their persons, houses, papers, and effects, against unreasonable searches and seizures, shall not be violated, and no Warrants shall issue, but upon probable cause, supported by Oath or affirmation, and particularly describing the place to be searched, and the persons or things to be seized.

Art. V

No person shall be held to answer for a capital, or otherwise infamous crime, unless on a presentment or indictment of a Grand Jury, except in cases arising in the land or naval forces, or in the Militia, when in actual service in time of War or public danger; nor shall any person be subject for the same offence to be twice put in jeopardy of life or limb, nor shall be compelled in any criminal case to be a witness against himself, nor be deprived of life, liberty, or property, without due process of law; nor shall private property be taken for public use, without just compensation.

Art. VI

In all criminal prosecutions, the accused shall enjoy the right to a speedy and public trial, by an impartial jury of the State and district wherein the crime shall have been committed, which district shall have been previously ascertained by law, and to be informed of the nature and cause of the accusation; to be confronted with the witnesses against him; to have compulsory process for obtaining witnesses in his favor, and to have the Assistance of Counsel for his defence.

Art. VII

In Suits at common law, where the value in controversy shall exceed twenty dollars, the right of trial by jury shall be preserved, and no fact tried by a jury, shall be otherwise re-examined in any Court of the United States, than according to the rules of the common law.

Art. VIII

Excessive bail shall not be required, nor excessive fines imposed, nor cruel and unusual punishments inflicted.

Art. IX

The enumeration in the Constitution, of certain rights, shall not be construed to deny or disparage others retained by the people.

Art. X

The powers not delegated to the United States by the Constitution, nor prohibited by it to the States, are reserved to the States respectively, or to the people.

JEFFERSON'S FIRST INAUGURAL ADDRESS
March 4, 1801

Friends and Fellow Citizens:

Called upon to undertake the duties of the first executive office of our country, I avail myself of the presence of that portion of my fellow citizens which is here assembled to express my grateful thanks for the favor with which they have been pleased to look toward me, to declare a sincere consciousness that the task is above my talents, and that I approach it with those anxious and awful presentiments which the greatness of the charge and the weakness of my powers so justly inspire. A rising nation, spread over a wide and fruitful land, traversing all the seas with the rich productions of their industry, engaged in commerce with nations who feel power and forget right, advancing rapidly to destinies beyond the reach of mortal eye — when I contemplate these transcendent objects, and see the honor, the happiness, and the hopes of this beloved country committed to the issue and the auspices of this day, I shrink from the contemplation, and humble myself before the magnitude of the undertaking. Utterly, indeed, should I despair did not the presence of many whom I here see remind me that in the other high authorities provided by our Constitution I shall find resources of wisdom, of virtue, and of zeal on which to rely under all difficulties. To you, the gentlemen, who are charged with the sovereign functions of legislation, and to those associated with you, I look with encouragement for that guidance and support which may enable us to steer with safety the vessel in which we are all embarked amidst the conflicting elements of a troubled world.

During the contest of opinion through which we have passed the animation of discussions and of exertions has sometimes worn an aspect which might impose on strangers unused to think freely and to speak and to write what they think; but this being now decided by the voice of the nation, announced according to the rules of the Constitution, all will, of course, arrange themselves under the will of the law, and unite in common efforts for the common good. All, too, will bear in mind this sacred principle, that though the will of the majority is in all cases to prevail, that will to be rightful must be reasonable; that the minority possess their equal rights, which equal law must protect, and to violate would be oppression. Let us, then, fellow citizens, unite with one heart and one mind. Let us restore to social intercourse that harmony and affection without which liberty and even life itself are but dreary things. And let us reflect that, having banished from our land that religious intolerance under which mankind so long bled and suffered, we have yet gained little if we countenance a political intolerance as despotic, as wicked, and capable of as bitter and bloody persecutions. During the throes and convulsions of the ancient world, during the agonizing spasms of infuriated man, seeking through blood and slaughter his long lost liberty, it was not wonderful that the agitation of the billows should reach even this distant and peaceful shore; that this should be more felt and feared by some and less by others, and should divide opinions as to measures of safety. But every difference of opinion is not a difference of principle. We have called by different names brethren of the same principle. We are all Republicans, we are all Federalists. If there be any among us who would wish to dissolve this Union or to change its republican form, let them stand undisturbed as mouments of the safety with which error of opinion may be tolerated where reason is left free to combat it. I know, indeed, that some honest men fear that a republican government can not be strong, that this Government is not strong enough; but would the honest patriot, in the full tide of successful experiment, abandon a government which has so far kept us free and firm on the theoretic and visionary fear that this Government, the world's best hope, may by possibility want energy to preserve itself? I trust not. I believe this, on the contrary, the strongest Government on earth. I believe it the only one where every man, at the call of the law, would fly to the standard of the law, and would meet invasions of the public order as his own personal concern. Sometimes it is said that man can not be trusted with the government of himself. Can he, then, be trusted with the government of others? Or have we found angels in the forms of kings to govern him? Let history answer this question.

Let us, then, with courage and confidence pursue our own Federal and Republican principles, our attachment to union and representative government. Kindly separated by nature and a wide ocean from the exterminating havoc of one quarter of the globe; too high minded to endure the degradations of the others; possessing a chosen country, with room enough for our descendants to the thousandth and thousandth generation; entertaining a due sense of our equal right to the use of our own faculties, honor and confidence from our fellow citizens, resulting not from birth, but from lightened by a benign religion, professed, indeed, and practiced in various forms, yet all of them inculcating honesty, truth, temperance, gratitude, and the love of man; acknowledging and adoring an overruling Providence, which by all its dispensations proves that it delights in the happiness of man here and his greater happiness hereafter with all these blessings, what more is necessary to make us a happy and a prosperous people? Still one thing more, fellow citizens a wise and frugal Government, which shall restrain men from injuring one another, shall leave them otherwise free to regulate their own pursuits of industry and improvement, and shall not take from the mouth of labor the bread it has earned. This is the sum of good government, and this is necessary to close the circle of our felicities.

About to enter, fellow citizens, on the exercise of duties which comprehend everything dear and valuable to you, it is proper you should understand what I deem the essential principles of our Government, and consequently those which ought to shape its Administration. I will compress them within the narrowest compass they will bear, stating the general principle, but not all its limitations. Equal and exact justice to all men, of whatever state of persuasion, religious or political: peace, commerce, and honest friendship with all nations, entangling alliances with none; the support of the State governments in all their rights, as the most competent administrations for our domestic concerns and the surest bulwarks against antirepublican tendencies; the preservation of the General Government in its whole constitutional vigor, as the sure anchor of our peace at home and safety abroad; a jealous care of the right of election by the people a mild and safe corrective of abuses which are lopped by the sword of revolution where peaceable remedies are unprovided; absolute acquiescence in the decisions of the majority, the vital principle and immediate parent of despotism; a well disciplined militia, our best reliance in peace and for the first moments of war, till regulars may relieve them; the supremacy of the civil public expense, that labor may be lightly burdened; the honest payment of our debts and sacred preservation of the public faith; encouragement of agriculture, and of commerce as its handmaid; the diffusion of information and arraignment of all abuses at the bar of the public reason; freedom of the press, and freedom of person under the protection of the habeas corpus, and trial by juries impartially selected. These principles form the bright constellation which has gone before us and guided our steps through an age of revolution and reformation. The wisdom of our sages and blood of our heroes have been devoted to their attainment. They should be devoted to their attainment. They should be the creed of our political faith, the text of civic instruction, the touchstone by which to try the services of those we trust; and should we wander from them in moments of error or of alarm, let us hasten to retrace our steps and to regain the road which alone adds to peace, liberty, and safety.

I repair, then, fellow citizens, to the post you have assigned me. With experience enough in subordinate offices to have seen the difficulties of this the greatest of all. I have learnt to expect that it will rarely fall to the lot of imperfect man to retire from this station with the reputation and the favor which bring him into it. Without pretensions to that high confidence you reposed in our first and greatest revolutionary character, whose preeminent services had entitled him to the first place in his country's love and destined for him the fairest page in the volume of faithful history, I ask so much confidence only as may give firmness and effect to the legal administration of your affairs. I shall often go wrong through defect of judgment. When right, I shall often be thought wrong by those whose positions will not command a view of the whole ground. I ask your indulgence for my own errors, which will never be intentional, and your support against the errors of others, who may condemn what they would not if seen in all its parts. The approbation implied by your suffrage is a great consolation to me for the past, and my future solicitude will be to retain the good opinion of those who have bestowed it in advance, to conciliate that of others by doing them all the good in my power, and to be instrumental to the happiness and freedom of all.

Relying, then, on the patronage of your good will, I advance with obedience to the work, ready to retire from it whenever you become sensible how much better choice it is in your power to make. And may that Infinite Power which rules the destinies of the universe lead our councils to what is best, and give them a favorable issue for your peace and prosperity.

The Gettysburg Address
November 19, 1863

Four score and seven years ago our fathers brought forth on this continent, a new nation, conceived in Liberty, and dedicated to the proposition that all men are created equal.

Now we are engaged in a great civil war, testing whether that nation or any nation so conceived and so dedicated, can long endure. We are met on a great battlefield of that war. We have come to dedicate a portion of that field as a final resting place for those who here gave their lives that that nation might live. It is altogether fitting and proper that we should do this.

But, in a larger sense, we can not dedicate–we cannot consecrate–we cannot hallow–this ground. The brave men, living and dead, who struggled here, have consecrated it far above our poor power to add or detract. The world will little note, nor long remember what we say here, but it can never forget what they did here. It is for us the living, rather, to be dedicated here to the unfinished work which they who fought here have thus far so nobly advanced. It is rather for us to be here dedicated to the great task remaining before us–that from these honored dead we take increased devotion to that cause for which they gave the last full measure of devotion–that we here highly resolve that these dead shall not have died in vain–that this nation, under God, shall have a new birth of freedom–and that government of the people, by the people, for the people, shall not perish from the earth.

The 19th Amendment to the Constitution of the United States giving women the right to vote August 26, 1920

Art. XIX

The right of citizens of the United States to vote shall not be denied or abridged by the United States or by any States on account of sex.

The Congress shall have power by appropriate legislation to enforce the provisions of this article.

DECLARATION OF INDEPENDENCE
OF THE DEMOCRATIC REPUBLIC
OF VIET-NAM
(September 2, 1945)

All men are created equal; they are endowed by their Creator with certain unalienable Rights; among these are Life, Liberty, and the pursuit of Happiness.

This immortal statement was made in the Declaration of Independence of the United States of America in 1776. In a broader sense, this means: All the peoples on the earth are equal from birth, all the peoples have a right to live, to be happy and free.

The Declaration of the French Revolution made in 1791 on the Rights of Man and the Citizen also states: "All men are born free and with equal rights, and must always remain free and have equal rights."

Those are undeniable truths.

Nevertheless, for more than eighty years, the French imperialists, abusing the standard of Liberty, Equality, and Fraternity, have violated our Fatherland and oppressed our fellow citizens. They have acted contrary to the ideals of humanity and justice.

In the field of politics, they have deprived our people of every democratic liberty.

They have enforced inhuman laws; they have set up three distinct political regimes in the North, the Center, and the South of Viet-Nam in order to wreck our national unity and prevent our people from being united.

They have built more prisons than schools. They have mercilessly slain our patriots; they have drowned our uprisings in rivers of blood.

They have fettered public opinion; they have practiced obscurantism against our people.

To weaken our race they have forced us to use

opium and alcohol.

In the field of economics, they have fleeced us to the backbone, impoverished our people and devastated our land.

They have robbed us of our rice fields, our mines, our forests, and our raw materials. They have monopolized the issuing of bank notes and the export trade.

They have invented numerous unjustifiable taxes and reduced our people, especially our peasantry, to a state of extreme poverty.

They have hampered the prospering of our national bourgeoisie; they have mercilessly exploited our workers.

In the autumn of 1940, when the Japanese fascists violated Indochina's territory to establish new bases in their fight against the Allies, the French imperialists went down on their bended knees and handed over our country to them.

Thus, from that date, our people were subjected to the double yoke of the French and the Japanese. Their sufferings and miseries increased. The result was that, from the end of last year to the beginning of this year, from Quang Tri Province to the North of Viet-Nam, more than two million of our fellow citizens died from starvation. On March 9 [1945], the French troops were disarmed by the Japanese. The French colonialists either fled or surrendered, showing that not only were they incapable of "protecting" us, but that, in the span of five years, they had twice sold our country to the Japanese.

On several occasions before March 9, the Viet Minh League urged the French to ally themselves with it against the Japanese. Instead of agreeing to this proposal, the French colonialists so intensified their terrorist activities against the Viet Minh members that before fleeing they massacred a great number of our political prisoners detained at Yen Bay and Cao Bang.

Notwithstanding all this, our fellow citizens have always manifested toward the French a tolerant and humane attitude. Even after the Japanese Putsch of March, 1945, the Viet Minh League helped many Frenchmen to cross the frontier, rescued some of them from Japanese jails, and protected French lives and property.

From the autumn of 1940, our country had in fact ceased to be a French colony and had become a Japanese possession.

After the Japanese had surrendered to the Allies, our whole people rose to regain our national sovereignty and to found the Democratic Republic of Viet-Nam.

The truth is that we have wrested our independence from the Japanese and not from the French.

The French have fled, the Japanese have capitulated, Emperor Bao Dai has abdicated. Our people have broken the chains which for nearly a century have fettered them and have won independence for the Fatherland. Our people at the same time have overthrown the monarchic regime that has reigned supreme for dozens of centuries. In its place has been established the present Democratic Republic.

For these reasons, we, members of the Provisional Government, representing the whole Vietnamese people, declare that from now on we break off all relations of a colonial character with France; we repeal all the international obligation that France has so far subscribed to on behalf of Viet-Nam, and we abolish all the special rights the French have unlawfully acquired in our Fatherland.

The whole Vietnamese people, animated by a common purpose, are determined to fight to the bitter end against any attempt by the French colonialists to reconquer their country.

We are convinced that the Allied nations, which

at Teheran and San Francisco have acknowledged the principles of self-determination and equality of nations, will not refuse to acknowledge the independence of Viet-Nam.

A people who have courageously opposed French domination for more than eighty years, a people who have fought side by side with the Allies against the fascists during these last years, such a people must be free and independent.

For these reasons, we, members of the Provisional Government of the Democratic Republic of Viet-Nam, solemnly declare to the world that Viet-Nam has the right to be a free and independent country - and in fact it is so already. The entire Vietnamese people are determined to mobilize all their physical and mental strength, to sacrifice their lives and property in order to safeguard their independence and liberty.

TRUMAN'S CIVIL RIGHTS MESSAGE
February 2, 1948
(80th Congress, 2d Session, House Doc. No. 516)

To the Congress of the United States:

In the state of the Union message on January 7, 1948, I spoke of five great goals toward which we should strive in our constant effort to strengthen our democracy and improve the welfare of our people. The first of these is to secure fully our essential human rights. I am now presenting to the Congress my recommendations for legislation to carry us forward toward that goal.

This Nation was founded by men and women who sought these shores that they might enjoy greater freedom and greater opportunity than they had known before. The founders of the United States proclaimed to the world the American belief that all men are created equal, and that governments are instituted to secure the inalienable rights with which all men are endowed. In the Declaration of Independence and the Constitution of the United States they eloquently expressed the aspirations of all mankind for equality and freedom.

These ideals inspired the peoples of other lands, and their practical fulfillment made the United States the hope of the oppressed everywhere. Throughout our history men and women of all colors and creeds, of all races and religions, have come to this country to escape tyranny and discrimination. Millions strong, they have helped build this democratic Nation and have constantly reinforced our devotion to the great ideals of liberty and equality. With those who preceded them, they have helped to fashion and strengthen our American faith - a faith that can be simply stated:

> We believe that all men are created equal and that they have the right to equal justice under law.

We believe that all men have the right to freedom of thought and of expression and the right to worship as they please.

We believe that all men are entitled to equal opportunities for jobs, for homes, for good health, and for education.

We believe that all men should have a voice in their government, and that government should protect, not usurp, the rights of the people.

These are the basic civil rights which are the source and the support of our democracy.

Today the American people enjoy more freedom and opportunity than ever before. Never in our history has there been better reason to hope for the complete realization of the ideals of liberty and equality.

We shall not, however, finally achieve the ideals for which this Nation was founded so long as any American suffers discrimination as a result of his race, or religion, or color, or the land of origin of his forefathers.

Unfortunately there still are examples - flagrant examples - of discrimination which are utterly contrary to our ideals. Not all groups of our population are free from the fear of violence. Not all groups are free to live and work where they please or to improve their conditions of life by their own efforts. Not all groups enjoy the full privileges of citizenship and participation in the Government under which they live.

We cannot be satisfied until all our people have equal opportunities for jobs, for homes, for education, for health, and for political expression, and until all our people have equal protection under the law....

The protection of civil rights is the duty of every

government which derives its powers from the consent of the people. This is equally true of local, State, and National Governments. There is much that the States can and should do at this time to extend their protection of civil rights. Wherever the law-enforcement measures of State and local governments are inadequate to discharge this primary function of government, these measures should be strengthened and improved.

The Federal Government has a clear duty to see that constitutional guaranties of individual liberties and of equal protection under the laws are not denied or abridged anywhere in our Union. That duty is shared by all three branches of the Government, but it can be fulfilled only if the Congress enacts modern, comprehensive civil rights laws, adequate to the needs of the day, and demonstrating our continuing faith in the free way of life.

I recommend, therefore, that the Congress enact legislation at this session directed toward the following specific objectives:

1. Establishing a permanent Commission on Civil Rights, a Joint Congressional Committee on Civil Rights, and a Civil Rights Division in the Department of Justice.

2. Strengthening existing civil rights statutes.

3. Providing Federal protection against lynching.

4. Protecting more adequately the right to vote.

5. Establishing a Fair Employment Practice Commission to prevent unfair discrimination in employment.

6. Prohibiting discrimination in interstate transportation facilities.

7. Providing home rule and suffrage in Presidential elections for the residents of the District of Columbia.

8. Providing statehood for Hawaii and Alaska and a greater measure of self-government for our island possessions.

9. Equalizing the opportunities for residents of the United States to become naturalized citizens.

10. Settling the evacuation claims of Japanese-Americans....

The legislation I have recommended for enactment by the Congress at the present session is a minimum program if the Federal Government is to fulfill its obligation of insuring the Constitutional guaranties of individual liberties and of equal protection under the law.

Under the authority of existing law the executive branch is taking every possible action to improve the enforcement of the civil rights statutes and to eliminate discrimination in Federal employment, in providing Federal services and facilities, and in the armed forces.

I have already referred to the establishment of the Civil Rights Division of the Department of Justice. The Federal Bureau of Investigation will work closely with this new Division in the investigation of Federal civil rights cases. Specialized training is being given to the Bureau's agents so that they may render more effective service in this difficult field of law enforcement.

It is the settled policy of the United States Government that there shall be no discrimination in Federal employment or in providing Federal services and facilities. Steady progress has been made toward this objective in recent years. I shall shortly issue an Executive order containing a comprehensive restatement of the Federal nondiscrimination policy, together with appropriate measures to ensure compliance.

During the recent war and in the years since its

close we have made much progress toward equality of opportunity in our armed services without regard to race, color, religion, or national origin. I have instructed the Secretary of Defense to take steps to have the remaining instances of discrimination in the armed services eliminated as rapidly as possible. The personnel policies and practices of all the services in this regard will be made consistent.

I have instructed the Secretary of the Army to investigate the status of civil rights in the Panama Canal Zone with a view to eliminating such discrimination as may exist there. If legislation is necessary, I shall make appropriate recommendations to the Congress....

The position of the United States in the world today makes it especially urgent that we adopt these measures to secure for all our people their essential rights.

The peoples of the world are faced with the choice of freedom or enslavement, a choice between a form of government which harnesses the state in the service of the individual and a form of government which chains the individual to the needs of the state.

We in the United States are working in company with other nations who share our desire for enduring world peace and who believe with us that, above all else, men must be free. We are striving to build a world family of nations - a world where men may live under governments of their own choosing and under laws of their own making.

As part of that endeavor, the Commission on Human Rights of the United Nations is now engaged in preparing an international bill of human rights by which the nations of the world may bind themselves by international covenant to give effect to basic human rights and fundamental freedoms. We have played a leading role in this undertaking designed to create a world order of law and justice fully protective of the rights and the dignity of the individual.

To be effective in these efforts , we must protect our civil rights so that by providing all our people with the maximum enjoyment of personal freedom and personal opportunity we shall be a stronger nation - stronger in our leadership, stronger in our moral position, stronger in the deeper satisfactions of a united citizenry.

We know that our democracy is not perfect. But we do know that it offers a fuller, freer, happier life to our people than any totalitarian nation has ever offered.

If we wish to inspire the peoples of the world whose freedom is in jeopardy, if we wish to restore hope to those who have already lost their civil liberties, if we wish to fulfill the promise that is ours, we must correct the remaining imperfections in our practice of democracy.

We know the way. We need only the will.

Harry S. Truman

Universal Declaration
of Human Rights

Preamble

Whereas recognition of the inherent dignity and of the equal and inalienable rights of all members of the human family is the foundation of freedom, justice and peace in the world,

Whereas disregard and contempt for human rights have resulted in barbarous acts which have outraged the conscience of mankind, and the advent of a world in which human beings shall enjoy freedom of speech and belief and freedom from fear and want has been proclaimed as the highest aspiration of the common people,

Whereas it is essential, if man is not to be compelled to have recourse, as a last resort, to rebellion against tyranny and oppression, that human rights should be protected by the rule of law,

Whereas it is essential to promote the development of friendly relations between nation,

Whereas the peoples of the United Nations have in the Charter reaffirmed their faith in fundamental human rights, in the dignity and worth of the human person and in the equal rights of men and women and have determined to promote social progress and better standards of life in larger freedoms,

Whereas Member States have pledged themselves to achieve, in co-operation with the United Nations, the promotion of universal respect for and observance of human rights and fundamental freedoms,

Whereas a common understanding of these rights and freedoms is of the greatest importance for the full realization of this pledge,

Now, Therefore,

THE GENERAL ASSEMBLY

proclaims

THIS UNIVERSAL DECLARATION OF HUMAN RIGHTS

as a common standard of achievement for all peoples and all nations, to the end that every individual and every organ of society, keeping this Declaration constantly in mind, shall strive by teaching and education to promote respect for these rights and freedoms and by progressive measures, national and international, to secure their universal and effective recognition and observance, both among the peoples of Member States themselves and among the peoples of territories under their jurisdiction.

Article 1

All human beings are born free and equal in dignity and rights. They are endowed with reason and conscience and should act towards one another in a spirit of brotherhood.

Article 2

Everyone is entitled to all the rights and freedoms set forth in this Declaration, without distinction of any kind, such as race, colour, sex, language, religion, political or other opinion, national or social origin, property, birth or other status.

Furthermore, no distinction shall be made on the basis of the political, jurisdictional or international status of the country or territory to which a person belongs, whether it be independent, trust, non-self-governing or under any other limitation of sovereignty.

Article 3

Everyone has the right to life, liberty and security of person.

Article 4

No one shall be held in slavery or servitude; slavery and the slave trade shall be prohibited in all their forms.

Article 5

No one shall be subjected to torture or to cruel, inhuman or degrading treatment or punishment.

Article 6

Everyone has the right to recognition everywhere as a person before the law.

Article 7

All are equal before the law and are entitled without any discrimination to equal protection of the law. All are entitled to equal protection against any discrimination in violation of this Declaration and against any incitement to such discrimination.

Article 8

Everyone has the right to an effective remedy by the competent national tribunals for acts violating the fundamental rights granted him by the constitution or law.

Article 9

No one shall be subjected to arbitrary arrest, detention or exile.

Article 10

Everyone is entitled in full equality to a fair and public hearing by an independent and impartial tribunal, in the determination of his rights and obligations and of any criminal charge against him.

Article 11

(1) Everyone charged with a penal offence has the right to be presumed innocent until proved guilty according to law in a public trial at which he has had all the guarantees necessary for his defence.

(2) No one shall be held guilty of any penal offence on account of any act or omission which did not constitute a penal offence, under national or international law, at the time when it was committed. Nor shall a heavier penalty be imposed than the one that was applicable at the time the penal offence was committed.

Article 12

No one shall be subjected to arbitrary interference with his privacy, family, home or correspondence, not to attacks upon his honour and reputation. Everyone has the right to the protection of the law against such interference or attacks.

Article 13

(1) Everyone has the right to freedom of movement and residence within the borders of each State.

(2) Everyone has the right to leave any country, including his own, and to return to his country.

Article 14

(1) Everyone has the right to seek and to enjoy in other countries asylum from persecution.

(2) This right may not be invoked in the case of prosecutions genuinely arising from non-political crimes or from acts contrary to the purposes and principles of the United Nations.

Article 15

(1) Everyone has the right to a nationality.

(2) No one shall be arbitrarily deprived of his nationality nor denied the right to change his nationality.

Article 16

(1) Men and women of full age, without any limitation due to race, nationality or religion, have the right to marry and to found a family. They are entitled to equal rights as to marriage, during marriage and at its dissolution.

(2) Marriage shall be entered into only with the free and full consent of the intending spouses.

(3) The family is the natural and fundamental group unit of society and is entitled to protection by society and the State.

Article 17

(1) Everyone has the right to own property alone as well as in association with others.

(2) No one shall be arbitrarily deprived of his property.

Article 18

Everyone has the right to freedom of thought, conscience and religion; this right includes freedom to change his religion or belief, and freedom, either alone or in community with others and in public or private, to manifest his religion or belief in teaching, practice, worship and observance.

Article 19

Everyone has the right to freedom of opinion and expression; this right includes freedom to hold opinions without interference and to seek, receive and impart information and ideas through any media and regardless of frontiers.

Article 20

(1) Everyone has the right to freedom of peaceful assembly and association.

(2) No one may be compelled to belong to an association.

Article 21

(1) Everyone has the right to take part in the government of his country, directly or through freely chosen representatives.

(2) Everyone has the right of equal access to public service in his country.

(3) The will of the people shall be the basis of the authority of government; this will shall be expressed in periodic and genuine elections which shall be by universal and equal suffrage and shall be held by secret vote or by equivalent free voting procedures.

Article 22

Everyone, as a member of society, has the right to social security and is entitled to realization, through national effort and international co-operation and in accordance with the organization and resources of each State, of the economic, social and cultural rights indispensable for his dignity and the free development of his personality.

Article 23

(1) Everyone has the right to work, to free choice of employment, to just and favourable conditions of work and to protection against unemployment.

(2) Everyone, without any discrimination, has the right to equal pay for equal work.

(3) Everyone who works has the right to just and favourable remuneration ensuring for himself and his family an existence worthy of human dignity, and supplemented, if necessary, by other means of social protection.

(4) Everyone has the right to form and to join trade unions for the protection of his interests.

Article 24

Everyone has the right to rest and leisure, including reasonable limitation of working hours and periodic holidays with pay.

Article 25

(1) Everyone has the right to a standard of living adequate for the health and well-being of himself and of his family, including food, clothing, housing and medical care and necessary social services, and the right to security in the event of unemployment, sickness, disability, widowhood, old age or other lack of livelihood in circumstances beyond his control.

(2) Motherhood and childhood are entitled to special care and assistance. All children, whether born in or out of wedlock, shall enjoy the same social protection.

Article 26

(1) Everyone has the right to education. Education shall be free, at least in the elementary and funda-

mental stages. Elementary education shall be compulsory. Technical and professional education shall
be made generally available and higher education
shall be equally accessible to all on the basis of
merit.

(2) Education shall be directed to the full development of the human personality and to the strengthening of respect for human rights and fundamental
freedoms. It shall promote understanding, tolerance
and friendship among all nations, racial or religious
groups, and shall further the activities of the United
Nations for the maintenance of peace.

(3) Parents have a prior right to choose the kind of
education that shall be given to their children.

Article 27

(1) Everyone has the right freely to participate in the
cultural life of the community, to enjoy the arts and
to share in scientific advancement and its benefits.

(2) Everyone has the right to the protection of the
moral and material interests resulting from any scientific, literary or artistic production of which he is
the author.

Article 28

Everyone is entitled to a social and international
order in which the rights and freedoms set forth in
this Declaration can be fully realized.

Article 29

(1) Everyone has duties to the community in which
alone the free and full development of his personality
is possible.

(2) In the exercise of his rights and freedoms, everyone shall be subject only to such limitations as are
determined by law solely for the purpose of securing

due recognition and respect for the rights and freedoms of others and of meeting the just requirements of morality, public order and the general welfare in a democratic society.

(3) These rights and freedoms may in no case be exercised contrary to the purposes and principles of the United Nations.

Article 30

Nothing in this Declaration may be interpreted as implying for any State, group or person any right to engage in any activity or to perform any act aimed at the destruction of any of the rights and freedoms set forth herein.

BROWN v. BOARD OF EDUCATION OF TOPEKA
347 U. S. 483
1954
Appeal from the U. S. District Court, District of Kansas.

WARREN, E. J. These cases come to us from the States of Kansas, South Carolina, Virginia, and Delaware. They are premised on different facts and different local conditions, but a common legal question justifies their consideration together in this consolidated opinion.

In each of the cases, minors of the Negro race, through their legal representatives, seek the aid of the courts in obtaining admission to the public schools of their community on a nonsegregated basis. In each instance, they have been denied admission to schools attended by white children under laws requiring or permitting segregation according to race. This segregation was alleged to deprive the plaintiffs of the equal protection of the laws under the Fourteenth Amendment. In each of the cases other than the Delaware case, a three-judge federal district court denied relief to the plaintiffs on the so-called "separate but equal" doctrine announced by this Court in Plessy v. Ferguson, 163 U. S. 537. Under that doctrine, equality of treatment is accorded when the races are provided substantially equal facilities, even though these facilities be separate. In the Delaware case, the Supreme Court of Delaware adhered to that doctrine, but ordered that the plaintiffs be admitted to the white schools because of their superiority to the Negro schools.

The plaintiffs contend that segregated public schools are not "equal" and cannot be made "equal," and that hence they are deprived of the equal protection of the laws. Because of the obvious importance of the question presented, the Court took jurisdiction. Argument was heard in the 1952 Term, and reargument was heard this Term on certain questions propounded by the Court.

Reargument was largely devoted to the circumstances surrounding the adoption of the Fourteenth Amendment in 1868. It covered exhaustively consideration of the Amendment in Congress, ratification by the states, then existing practices in racial segregation, and the views of proponents and opponents of the Amendment. This discussion and our own investigation convince us that, although these sources cast some light, it is not enough to resolve the problem with which we are faced. At best, they are inconclusive. The most avid proponents of the post-War Amendments undoubtedly intended them to remove all legal distinctions among "all persons born or naturalized in the United States." Their opponents, just as certainly, were antagonistic to both the letter and the spirit of the Amendments and wished them to have the most limited effect. What others in Congress and the state legislatures had in mind cannot be determined with any degree of certainty.

An additional reason for the inconclusive nature of the Amendment's history, with respect to segregated schools, is the status of public education at that time. In the South, the movement toward free common schools, supported by general taxation, had not yet taken hold. Education of white children was largely in the hands of private groups. Education of Negroes was almost nonexistent, and practically all of the race were illiterate. In fact, any education of Negroes was forbidden by law in some states. Today, in contrast, many Negroes have achieved outstanding success in the arts and sciences as well as in the business and professional world. It is true that public education had already advanced further in the North, but the effect of the Amendment on Northern States was generally ignored in the congressional debates. Even in the North, the conditions of public education did not approximate those existing today. The curriculum was usually rudimentary; ungraded schools were common in rural areas; the school term was but three months a year in many states; and compulsory school attendance was virtually unknown. As a consequence, it is not surprising that there should be so little in the history of the Fourteenth Amendment relating to its intended effect on public education.

In the first cases in this Court construing the Fourteenth Amendment, decided shortly after its adoption, the Court interpreted it as proscribing all state-imposed discriminations against the Negro race. The doctrine of "separate but equal" did not make its appearance in this Court until 1896 in the case of Plessy v. Ferguson, supra, involving not education but transportation. American courts have since labored with the doctrine for over half a century. In this Court, there have been six cases involving the "separate but equal" doctrine in the field of public education. In Cumming v. Board of Education of Richmond County, 175 U. S. 528, and Gong Lum v. Rice, 275 U. S. 78, the validity of the doctrine itself was not challenged. In more recent cases, all on the graduate school level, inequality was found in that specific benefits enjoyed by white students were denied to Negro students of the same educational qualifications. State of Missouri ex rel. Gaines v. Canada, 305 U. S. 337; Sipuel v. Board of Regents of University of Oklahoma, 332 U. S. 631; Sweatt v. Painter, 339 U. S. 629; McLaurin v. Oklahoma State Regents, 339 U. S. 637. In none of these cases was it necessary to reexamine the doctrine to grant relief to the Negro plaintiff. And in Sweatt v. Painter, supra, the Court expressly reserved decision on the question whether Plessy v. Ferguson should be held inapplicable to public education.

In the instant cases, that question is directly presented. Here, unlike Sweatt v. Painter, there are findings below that the Negro and white schools involved have been equalized, or are being equalized, with respect to buildings, curricula, qualifications and salaries of teachers, and other "tangible" factors. Our decision, therefore, cannot turn on merely a comparison of these tangible factors in the Negro and white schools involved in each of the cases. We must look instead to the effect of segregation itself on public education.

In approaching this problem, we cannot turn the clock back to 1868 when the Amendment was adopted, or even to 1896 when Plessy v. Ferguson was written. We must consider public education in the light of its full development and its present place in American life throughout the Nation. Only in this way can it be determined if segregation in public schools deprives these plaintiffs of the equal protection of the laws.

Today, education is perhaps the most important function of state and local governments. Compulsory school attendance laws and the great expenditures for education both demonstrate our recognition of the importance of education to our democratic society. It is required in the performance of our most basic public responsibilities, even service in the armed forces. It is the very foundation of good citizenship. Today it is a principal instrument in awakening the child to cultural values, in preparing him for later professional training, and in helping him to adjust normally to his environment. In these days, it is doubtful that any child may reasonably be expected to succeed in life if he is denied the opportunity of an education. Such an opportunity, where the state has undertaken to provide it, is a right which must be made available to all on equal terms.

We come then to the question presented: Does segregation of children in public schools solely on the basis of race, even though the physical facilities and other 'tangible' factors may be equal, deprive the children of the minority group of equal educational opportunities? We believe that it does.

In Sweatt v. Painter, supra [339 U. S. 629, 70

S.Ct. 850], in finding that a segregated law school for Negroes could not provide them equal educational opportunities, this Court relied in large part on "those qualities which are incapable of objective measurement but which make for greatness in a law school." In McLaurin v. Oklahoma State Regents, supra [339 U. S. 637, 70 S.Ct. 853], the Court, in requiring that a Negro admitted to a white graduate school be treated like all other students, again resorted to intangible consideration: "... his ability to study, to engage in discussions and exchange views with other students, and, in general, to learn his profession." Such considerations apply with added force to children in grade and high schools. To separate them from others of similar age and qualifications solely because of their race generates a feeling of inferiority as to their status in the community that may affect their hearts and minds in a way unlikely ever to be undone. The effect of this separation on their educational opportunities was well stated by a finding in the Kansas case by a court which nevertheless felt compelled to rule against the Negro plaintiffs:

"Segregation of white and colored children in public schools has a detrimental effect upon the colored children. The impact is greater when it has the sanction of the law; for the policy of separating the races is usually interpreted as denoting the inferiority of the Negro group. A sense of inferiority affects the motivation of a child to learn. Segregation with the sanction of law, therefore, has a tendency to retard the educational and mental development of Negro children and to deprive them of some of the benefits they would receive in a racially integrated school system."

Whatever may have been the extent of psychological knowledge at the time of Plessy v. Ferguson, this finding is amply supported by modern authority. Any language in Plessy v. Ferguson contrary to this finding is rejected.

We conclude that in the field of public education

the doctrine of "separate but equal" has no place. Separate educational facilities are inherently unequal. Therefore, we hold that the plaintiffs and others similarly situated for whom the actions have been brought are, by reason of the segregation complained of, deprived of the equal protection of the laws guaranteed by the Fourteenth Amendment. This disposition makes unnecessary any discussion whether such segregation also violates the Due Process Clause of the Fourteenth Amendment.

Because these are class actions, because of the wide applicability of this decision, and because of the great variety of local conditions, the formulation of decrees in these cases presents problems of considerable complexity. On reargument, the consideration of appropriate relief was necessarily subordinated to the primary question - the constitutionality of segregation in public education. We have now announced that such segregation is a denial of the equal protection of the laws. In order that we may have the full assistance of the parties in formulating decrees, the cases will be restored to the docket, and the parties are requested to present further argument....The Attorney General of the United States is again invited to participate. The Attorneys General of the states requiring or permitting segregation in public education will also be permitted to appear as amici curiae upon request to do so by September 15, 1954 and submission of briefs by October 1, 1954.

It is so ordered.

SPEECH BY HAILE SELASSIE

"What life has taught me I would like to share with those who want to learn

Until the philosophy which holds one race superior
and another inferior is finally and permanently
discredited and abandoned

that until there are no longer first class and
second class citizens of any nation
until the color of a man's skin is of no more
significance than the color of his eyes
that until these basic human rights are equally
guaranteed to all without regard to race

that until that day,
the dream of lasting peace, world citizenship and
the rule of international morality
will remain but a fleeting illusion
to be pursued, but never attained

and until the ignoble and unhappy regime that
hold
our brothers in Angola, in Mozambique, South
Africa
in sub-human bondage, have been toppled -
utterly destroyed

until that day the African continent will not know
peace
we Africans will fight if necessary
and we know we shall win
as we are confident in the victory of
good over evil, good over evil."

Speech by Haile Selassie

California

February 28, 1968